"In reading *Inside the Mind*, I have realized that the way I think is very different from others. This book has provided me with the words to explain these differences to my wife and family, so that they can start to understand me better. My wife has been frustrated with me for years and thought I was doing things on purpose to her that seemed rude. Also, when I did not answer her right away, she assumed I didn't care. With her understanding of IRI, she now realizes that there is a reason for what I am doing, and I have not intentionally been hurtful to her. She has been able to become more patient for me to process information and respond to her. I have also been able to gain the confidence to ask her to explain to me what she thinks are obvious and simple social cues so that I can be more socially appropriate."

For those who have inductive reasoning issues or have family members with it, this book will go a long way to helping explain the world of Inductive Reasoning.

Brad G. – born with IRI

"Learning about IRI has really helped me understand my kids. The assumptions I used to make, based on how my brain is wired, interfered with my connection to them. This book taught me how to communicate directly, specifically, and concretely with my kids. I found this book very comprehensive and useful as a parent with practical tools to work with the kids, which really improved our relationship. It's a great book!"

Birgitte V. – parent

"I cried as I read this book. It's the first time I thought someone understood me. I thought, 'Oh my God! I'm not the only person who has a gazillion boxes that have no labels on them!' This book helped me understand that things can be very connected for me but I organize things differently than others."

Katie C. – head injury when young

"This book gave me valuable insights into how people with IRI experience the world around them. The concepts and examples are clear and practical and helped me improve my communication and ability to have healthy relationships with important people in my life."

Molly B. – parent

"As I read Suzanne's book, I discovered new ways to frame experiences with my children. Her book challenged me to think outside the small set of labels that had been used to describe my child's behavior and see more positive ways to think about how I parent. Her book was very helpful in changing my definitions of ADHD and anxiety."

Marjorie B. – parent

"This book is so gentle in its presentation. There is no judgment, just understanding. I plan to give it to my step-daughter to read so that she might understand herself better."

Gwen A. – step-parent

"I found this book very comprehensive and useful as a parent. It's well organized with clear guidance on how to communicate and work with someone who has inductive reasoning issues. It's a great tool!"

Margaret A. – parent

Inside the Mind

Understanding and Communicating with Those Who Have Autism, Asperger's, Social Communication Disorder, and ADD

Suzanne D. Morris, MA, LMFT

Book Publishers Network
Changing the World One Book at a Time

Book Publishers Network
P.O. Box 2256
Bothell • WA • 98041
Ph • 425-483-3040
www.bookpublishersnetwork.com

10 9 8 7 6 5 4 3 2 1

Printed in the United States of America

LCCN 2016937779
ISBN 978-1-940598-99-4

Editor: Julie Scandora
Cover designer: Laura Zugzda
Layout: Melissa Vail Coffman

Contents

Introduction ix

Chapter 1: Inductive Reasoning. 1
Understanding Inductive Reasoning Issues 4
Experiencing Inductive Reasoning Issues 7
Levels of Inductive Reasoning Issues 9
Introverts and Extroverts 13
Feelers and Thinkers 16
How to Use This Book. 20

Chapter 2: Understanding Aspects of Inductive Reasoning Issues 25
Eye Contact 26
Body Language of Others. 30
Body Awareness of Self 31
Improving Body Awareness and Increasing Relaxation . . 33
Making Meaning 37
Translating Meaning to Other Situations or Other Environments 39
Grouping Similar Things 42
Empathy 47
Understanding and Caring about Others 45
Their Impact on Others 47
Learning from Past Experiences 54
Initiating 55

Asking for Help 56
Thinking Differently or Divergent Thinkers 61
Literal 62
Perfectionist 66
Resistance to Change—Possible OCD 67
Imagination 69
Memory 72
Attention 75
Organization 80
Time Awareness 82
Over-Focus 84
Lack of Focus 86
Mega-rules, Rules, and Sub-rules 88
Behavior Issues 91
Defining Feelings 92
Stress, Worry, Fear, Anxiety, and Panic 98
Frustration 106
Depression 107
Confusion 113
Teens and Their Development 114
Ways of Coping 117
Gaming. .117
Taking on a Role. 120
Down Time 121
Down Time Ideas 122
Communication. 125
Colloquialisms and Idioms 128
Sensory Issues 130
Sensory Overload or Lack of Filters 130
Over-stimulating Environments 135
Listening to Those with Sensory Overload 139
Other Sensory Issues 141

Highly Sensitive People vs. IRI 143
Sixth Sense and Safety 144

Chapter 3: Additional Health Issues 147
What Causes IRI, Autism, Asperger's, Social Communication Disorder, and ADD? 147
Genetics .147
Brain Trauma. 148
Sleep Issues 149
Vision Issues 151
Nutrition 151
Toxins 154
Cell Phones, Cell Tower Antennas, Wi-Fi, and Electromagnetic Frequencies 154

Chapter 4: Diagnosing 157
Diagnosing IRI 159
Signs of IRI 159
Social Communication Disorder 163
Asperger's Syndrome or Autism 164
Other Diagnostic Tools 165
Gifted or IRI or Both 167
Differential Diagnosis 169
Doing Psychotherapy or Counseling 171

Chapter 5: Working with Those Who Have Inductive Reasoning Issues 175
Basic Guidelines for Us to Help Them 175
Scaling Anything 176
Working with Children Who Have IRI 177
Working with Teens Who Have IRI 178
Working with Adults Who Have IRI 178
Working with Parents of Those Who Have IRI 179

Working with Partners of Those Who Have IRI 181
Working with Couples or Partners Together 181
Working with Families with One Who Has IRI 182
Working with Teachers of Students with IRI 182
Working with Children of Those Who Have IRI 184
Final Overview 185

Resources 187
Getting Help 187
Types of Therapists and Doctors 189
Types of Therapy and What They Address 194
Grief Information 198
Phases of Grief Outline 199
Phases of Grief Explained 202

Books, DVDs, Games, and Other Resources 213
Books 213
Children's Books with Social Themes. 227
DVDs, Other Recordings, Movies, and TV 230
Social Skills Games 233
Online Resources 237

Worksheets and Instructions 239

Index 251

Introduction

In 2008, I was told a family member had aspects of Asperger's but not enough to get that diagnosis. I read several books on Asperger's syndrome, but most of it didn't fit. The psychologist also told me my family member couldn't do inductive reasoning well. Most of us know what *deductive reasoning* is—finding all the details in a story. But like everyone else I know, I had no clue what *inductive reasoning* really meant. We do it all the time but are unaware that we are doing it. The psychologist told me my family member struggled to put pieces of information together to make meaning. OK, so that's the definition, but what does it really mean in everyday life for the people who have it? And how do I relate better to them? I went home and looked up what I could on inductive reasoning and found little other than the dictionary definition. So I spent some months thinking intently about it and watching my family members.

After a year of reading and struggling to understand, I sat one day and looked around my office and said to myself, "If I saw everything as an individual piece of information without any connections to each other or to me, what would that be like?" Somehow I was given the gift of my brain making that leap for several moments, and I suddenly experienced everything as an individual piece of information. Everything went emotionally flat when there was no meaning attached. And without meaning or a way to group things, I was astounded and totally overwhelmed by the amount of information present and my inability to organize or filter it. This book is the culmination of what I figured out about that experience, my understanding from multiple family members who struggle with inductive reasoning, as well as my professional experience and understanding in working with those who have social communication disorder, Asperger's syndrome (now autism), autism, or ADD. Those with ADHD, anxiety, social phobia, narcissism, and bipolar can also struggle with inductive reasoning issues.

I wrote this book to help people understand how those who have inductive reasoning issues (IRI) process information. My hope is that, once you understand IRI, everyone's frustration level will be lower, and there will be better communication in families, schools, and work places. I also hope that family members who don't have it can understand that those who do have it are not behaving out of choice. They are often not trying to be unkind or uncaring. They are often quiet when they don't understand. They can't do empathy well or, for some, at all. My hope is that you don't take their behavior personally, or you will suffer when you don't need to suffer.

I grew up with a parent who has it. He was a quiet, unassuming man. He was a teacher who remembered everyone's name and was well liked by everyone. I don't remember my father ever initiating any conversation with me. He was open when I went to him, but he never asked me how I was doing, what I was doing, how I was feeling, etc. He acted very uncomfortable whenever I shared my feelings with him, and he had no response to them. My interpretation of his behavior was that I was not important to him and that he really didn't care about me. It took me many years to overcome that. It was true that he didn't understand me or know how to respond to me but for very different reasons than what I thought. My hope is that families will come to understand IRI and that children and partners won't have to go through the pain I experienced. Or, if you have had a similar experience, this book will help you let go of it. I didn't figure out my dad had IRI until he was eighty-nine. And I didn't figure out *how* to talk with him until I figured out he had it. Finally our relationship is working better. So never give up!

For those raising children who have this issue, you can teach them a lot. This book can help you understand the way they process information. You will have to be specific in your words and explanations, or they will not understand what you are trying to teach them. And they won't be able to tell you they don't understand. This book can help you to change your expectations for them and let go of many unrealistic expectations, especially if you want a relationship where you can really meet and connect with them where they live. It's like learning a different language in a culture that is very different from yours. I encourage you to keep working through your grief and focus on helping your child, instead of becoming lost in discouragement or frustration. Children with IRI still have a full life ahead of them, and you don't know where they will end up.

Get support for yourself whether you are a parent, partner, or child of someone who has IRI. It's important to keep working through your grief and frustration and not get stuck in it. That is why I included some information on the grief process in the resource section. Elisabeth Kubler-Ross did a great service to all with her information about grief for those who are dying. For those who are living, there is a different process that includes searching behavior and often not bargaining. There is information about that in the grief section. I encourage family members to figure out ways to get your emotional needs met that are creative and may be from others outside the family.

For teachers and bosses, students and employees need very specific information on expectations for their work. Asking them if they heard you or understand you won't work. They can often parrot back exactly what you said. Checking with them about *what they understand* they are supposed to do and *how* they are supposed to do it will help you learn how they think. It will allow you to correct them before they attempt things. It will allow them to show you what they really know or can do instead of making mistakes that are based on misinterpretation. It will also train you on how you need to word your expectations so they can meet them. I'm willing to talk to groups about inductive reasoning issues.

For psychotherapists, the lack of inductive reasoning is the cause for a diagnosis of social communication disorder. Lack of inductive reasoning, along with high focus, was the key to an Asperger's diagnosis, which is now listed as autism. Those with autism have this issue. I believe that many people diagnosed with ADD, ADHD, anxiety, social phobia, reactive attachment disorder, bipolar, or narcissism have IRI. I think it is missed a lot in those who I define as Level 4s. I consult with others on cases, and I plan to do training that will help professionals understand and be able to word things in ways that allow them to get the information they need and help those with IRI get what they need. I'm also willing to talk to groups about inductive reasoning issues.

For those who have IRI, I hope this book helps you understand more about what you deal with every day and why you feel so stressed or anxious. I hope it helps you to understand why others get so frustrated with you and why you get frustrated with them. I also hope you learn ways to manage or lower your stress that are helpful. I may write a book with specific information about understanding those who don't have IRI so you can better understand the majority of people in the world.

It took me a long time to finish this book because I initially wrote it for the those who can do inductive reasoning. I then went back and rewrote it many times to clear all the idioms and colloquialisms, writing out the full meaning of what I was saying, instead of using words that could be more easily misinterpreted, and making it readable for those with IRI. It was a grueling process that really taught me how to talk with those who have IRI. And it really gave me a better understanding of how hard they work to understand others.

I invite you to visit my website, www.Counsel-Heal.com, for other information. I have video clips on YouTube of a few things from this book. My next task is a video of the information in the first chapter of this book for auditory/visual learners as well as part of continuing education for therapists and teachers. That will be available on my website when it is finished. I hope to have an audio book of this book out by the end of 2016 for those of you who are auditory learners. I have plans for additional books on feelings, communication, parenting, rules, and one on aspects of several diagnoses and how to deal with them from a variety of modalities and not only traditional talk counseling. I may write about my experiences growing up and how I healed. We'll see how many books I do write and how soon I can get them done. I didn't realize how long the process took for writing and getting them published, as well as the costs involved! *Please be respectful of how much time and energy it took for me to write this book. Please also respect the copyright and ask for permission in writing to use anything in this book that is not for personal use once you have bought this book.*

I hope this book is helpful to you all and healing to some. My heart goes out to all who are dealing with this issue.

Blessings!

Chapter 1 | Inductive Reasoning

You may have skipped the introduction, as I usually do, but I highly encourage you to go back and read it. I've shared how this book came into being and the reason I wrote it, which will impact your reading of it.

Here are common things that are said by others about those with inductive reasoning issues (IRI.) If you have said these things in your own mind or to others, you may be dealing with someone who has IRI.

- Why do they act that way?
- What is wrong with them?
- They are weird or that was weird.
- I just explained things. Why don't they get it?
- They are so frustrating to deal with!
- I'm really uncomfortable. They are doing strange things, and I don't know how to respond. I just want to get away.

Parents talking about their children might think the following.

- I've told them that a million times, and they just don't listen!!
- I don't understand what their problem is or what to do to help them.
- They don't care about anyone but themselves!

- I really worry about them because they don't seem to have any friends. All they do is play computer games in their room.
- They will never make it in the real world!

Here are some things that those with inductive reasoning issues say to themselves:

- I don't understand what they are asking me.
- I don't understand what just happened. Why are they mad at me? I didn't say anything wrong.
- I just did what they asked me to. What is their problem?
- I feel anxious or uncomfortable and I don't know why!
- I don't understand what others are doing. I don't understand why they are doing it. Why do they get in small groups and talk (on the playground, after school, after church)?
- I don't know what to say to other people.
- No one seems to understand me. It is so frustrating!
- People are usually wrong about what I think or why I am doing something. And when I explain it to them, they don't understand. Why don't they understand me?

Here are some behaviors that may indicate that a person struggles with IRI.

- Lacks eye contact
- Is clumsy
- Struggles to hold a pencil to write
- Doesn't gesture
- Lacks facial expression
- Lacks empathy (but may be very caring)

- Is totally honest
- Is tactless
- Is unaware of how his or her behavior affects others
- Lacks friends
- Lacks imagination
- Struggles to understand what others mean
- Doesn't ask for help
- Is literal
- Perfectionist
- Likes routine, doesn't like new things
- Resists change
- Has an amazing memory for facts
- Follows the rules
- Struggles with others who don't follow the rules
- Only focuses on one thing
- Lacks time awareness
- Prefers to be alone
- Seems to have no filters
- Only eats the same foods
- Is overly sensitive to lights, sounds, tastes, textures

Most of these behaviors were common to an Asperger's syndrome diagnosis in the past. Now there is a diagnosis of social communication disorder, or some people use non-verbal learning disorder, which addresses the struggle with pragmatic language skills. But this doesn't explain how their mind works or how they process information. Hopefully this book will help you to understand and to communicate with those who struggle with inductive reasoning issues.

Understanding Inductive Reasoning Issues

People who have inductive reasoning issues (IRI) are affected in several ways. They all stem from the inability to move from the details to the larger picture, to put detailed information together to form meaning, to easily prioritize and organize what they see and hear into information that is helpful.

The dictionary says inductive reasoning is the process of reasoning or drawing a conclusion from particular facts. Most of us walk into a room and note some things in the room. We automatically sort what we see or hear into things that we like or that we are curious about or that we don't care about. The things that we like, the things we are curious about, and the things we don't care about will all have different priorities. We will move the information into short-term or long-term memory based on our interests and priorities. When others are present, we see/hear a group of body cues (facial expression, body movements or how people hold their body, and tones in the voice) and we make the inductive reasoning leap of defining that group of body cues as a single meaning about how they are feeling. We attach a level of importance to the meaning about it that allows us to store and recover that information or memory easily. And we do it all without consciously thinking about it. It happens for us in a moment or two.

But what if you have IRI? What does it mean in a practical sense if you can't put details together to make meaning? Here is an illustration that may help you understand how information is received, processed, and stored for someone who has *severe* IRI.

Imagine that your mind is a huge personal warehouse of boxes with files. You have a file of information on every person or situation or place you encounter, which you place in a box in the warehouse. This is how you use and store your files.

Whenever you enter a new room, you create a file for that room and log everything in that room in that file. Each time you enter that room, you pull the file for that room, and you notice if your file matches what's in the room. If there is anything new or missing or changed, you log the change for future reference. There is no interpretation of why the room has the items in it or looks the way it looks. Nothing in the room has any priority or meaning, other than it is in that room. There's no personal reaction or connection to the items in the room or connection to the room itself. You just keep a running list of things.

Each time you meet a person, you create a file and note every detail you can about that person. Every time you see them you pull their file and add information. There is no interpretation about that person. You note their lip went up or down when they said a certain thing. Their eyebrows rose when you said a certain thing. You have no clue what that means; you just note that it happened. You are so busy logging everything that you may not speak until you are spoken to. And your response may not be appropriate to the person or situation since all you are doing is noting the details without any meaning or connection to them. Again, you keep a running list of things.

When you are done logging details, you place the labeled file in a box that isn't labeled in the warehouse. Within a box, you might have a person file with a place file with a situation file. There are no similarities or connections between the files, even though they are in the same box.

You place the box anywhere you can find room for the box in the warehouse on a shelf that isn't labeled. You may pile boxes on top of other boxes, but there is no organization to the boxes.

Unless you have a single focus, which many on the autism spectrum experience, there is no designated area in your warehouse for a topic. If you have an intense interest, you may shove everything to the sides and place the boxes on your topic in the front and center. You will keep adding more and more files in more and more boxes on your topic of intense interest and ignore all the other files in boxes, unless you are required to shift focus.

When you have IRI and are asked for information about a person, place, or situation, you enter the warehouse of your mind. But there is no organization to anything. The shelves or boxes aren't labeled or grouped by place, person, or situation. There are no levels of shelves or stacks of boxes based on priority, interest, number of times used, etc. The boxes are placed based on the time you finished filling that box. But you have a prodigious memory that allows you to weave through all the boxes to just the right one and pull the file you are looking for from that box. But it might take you a little longer to find that file than it would take for others to access a file in their warehouse.

When you try to access information from that file, you will struggle. When you cannot make meaning, then there is no reference within a file to other things in the file. You do not group things that are similar. It's just a list. So you have to take the time to scan through the file for the information.

There are no references in the file to other files anywhere in the warehouse. So, there is no cross-reference system in the warehouse because nothing is organized. Nothing is labeled, except the file, nothing is noted to be similar to any other thing, and nothing has any meaning. There is no keyword search for a topic or grouping of behavior or experiences. *The only search engine is word specific for the title of the file.*

If you are feeling overwhelmed reading this explanation, then you know what those with IRI feel like *all the time.* If you wonder why you are so anxious and think you might have IRI, this might give you some insight into the reasons.

Because it takes you a little longer than others to figure out the file needed and then to access the information that is requested from that file, you appear a little slow to respond. Others may become impatient with you or think you are slow or stupid. There are times you aren't sure what information people are asking for. You might guess and pull the wrong file and give the wrong answer, which confuses other people. Some people may ridicule you. Or you can't figure out what file to pull so you don't know how to answer the question. Internally, you may keep searching for what you think might be the right file and take a long time to respond. Or you may finally give up and never respond. Others will be confused or angry depending on how they interpret your lack of response. If you don't see the point in finding the file, you won't ever respond. Others may give up trying to relate to you if they don't get a response of some kind.

> **Inductive Reasoning** is being able to group pieces of information to make meaning and storing them based on priority, interest, or use so you know how to remember the information and how to respond to it. Those with IRI often take in information as single pieces of data that aren't connected. They struggle to connect information. And they can take longer to respond.

Experiencing Inductive Reasoning Issues

If you are someone who can do inductive reasoning and you want to try to experience what this is like, here is an exercise you can do. Take a seat in a room. Set a timer for three minutes. Try to name everything in the room out loud as fast as you can without thinking about the item you are naming. Your goal is to name as many things as you can in three minutes. Go!

Whew! Did you get very far? How quickly did you feel overwhelmed or slow down? Did you find you had any time to relate to anything you were naming? How many times were you pulled to stop to think about the item or something similar you remembered? If you did, try it again until you have no connection to the items.

That is the closest I believe those who can do inductive reasoning can come to the experience of not being able to do inductive reasoning.

Now, imagine there is more than one person in the room interacting. Think how fast you would be logging information and how much you might miss as you shift focus from one person to another. Do you have any time to think of something to say, or has the topic shifted by the time you are ready to say something?

Now, imagine you are in a classroom with thirty kids and a teacher or in a business meeting. Whom would you track and when? How hard would it be to try to figure out what information was important?

What would you miss just trying to answer that question for yourself? How can you track multiple people and many interactions? How overloaded would you be trying to track everyone? What is important information when you can't attach meaning to details?

Now, imagine you are in an assembly of hundreds at school or at the mall. You don't know what to *not* track. You are trying to log everything and are now on information overload to the max!

The information gathering jumps exponentially as the number in the group increases. Information is passing back and forth so quickly that those with IRI can get lost. You can't watch every person in a detailed way all the time. It becomes a mass of input that can't be logged anymore because it's moving so fast and among so many people that one can't keep track. You either pick only a few people to really log (like the person running the class or assembly) or *you withdraw and give up—which is a totally normal response to information overload and is, in fact, helpful to the nervous system.*

We need to learn to wait patiently for those with IRI to respond. If given twice the normal time and they don't respond, then we should ask them what they are thinking. Or ask them what they understand the question to be. If they repeat exactly what we said, that does not mean they understand. I will talk more about this in the communication section under "Aspects of Inductive Reasoning Issues."

Experiencing IRI

Sit in a room and try to name as many objects in the room as you can in three minutes without thinking about the objects. Don't stop to think about them or have any feelings about them. Just list them out loud.

Those with IRI are often on information overload, and that is what organizes their behavior. We need to be patient and helpful to them. They need time and help to process for the correct meaning and use of the information they are logging.

Levels of Inductive Reasoning Issues

There is a continuum from no IRI to extreme IRI. In order to help you understand where you or others might be, I've organized levels of IRI based on the impact that it has on processing information and the impact that it has on relationships. This can help you sort out what is needed in relating to those with IRI or what they need in order to relate to those who can do inductive reasoning. I reference introvert or extrovert in the levels, which I will explain in more detail after the levels section.

Level 1 – High Impact

People who are highly impacted by IRI don't have any, or many, verbal skills and need significant intervention growing up. They need constant oversight as children and often significant oversight as adults. *I'm not addressing that population in this book, but reading the book may give you insight into their struggle.*

Level 2 – Major Impact, Not Aware of Others

This population will need a lot of training and then ongoing coaching to become socially appropriate. They don't realize that others have different thoughts and feelings than they do until someone points it out to them. And then they won't understand why others think or feel differently, but they may come to accept, with coaching, that others *do* think and feel differently. But they will struggle to know how to use that information to create or manage relationships.

They don't know how to join or leave a conversation. They work at social skills because those in authority tell them to do it. They may not have a lot of internal motivation to interact with others. They will do it to follow the rules of their parents or teachers. They will participate with family at holidays because that is the rule or they have always done it. They may not understand the importance of friends but may choose to do things with people based on the same interest. They generally don't want to interact with others unless people are talking about something they are really interested in. If they aren't, then they don't understand why people are talking about something that is sooooo boring! It's clear to others that those with Level 2 IRI don't understand things, and often people will just say, "That's the way they are," and not be offended by the behavior, or people may just ignore them.

Those with IRI at this level may find jobs in their area of interest that don't require them to interact a lot with people and will survive as adults. They may look and sound very logical most of the time, but it will be their own logic and not the logic of those who can do inductive reasoning. They may become more interested in friends later in life if they move towards Level 3 and will need significant ongoing coaching to be socially appropriate.

Level 3 – Moderate Impact, Sometimes Aware of Others or Themselves

People in this group will need a lot of training and coaching to become socially appropriate, but they will work hard at it. They usually want friends. When they try to make friends, they make many social mistakes that are apparent when they are young. They come to understand they need help and they need to work at it if they are going to have friends. They often listen carefully and work hard to learn appropriate behavior and rules about interacting with others. They may be willing to tell others that they struggle with social cues, and so friends may be more patient or tease in fun ways. But peers will still get irritated at times and still be unkind or bully them when they are children.

Those that are more logical and/or rigid will struggle more with others when other people have behavior that is not fitting the rules they have figured out about the world. Or they will struggle more when the rules change because rules do change as people grow up. They may struggle with understanding and keeping in mind that there are different rules for family, for friends/peers, for adults, bosses, partners, etc.

Level 4 – Minor Impact, Somewhat Aware of Others or Themselves

People on Level 4 need training and coaching and a lot of support. These folks work very hard to appear normal. They get some of the body/social cues but miss some that are more nuanced. This can cause them to be tentative or withdrawn in social situations, whether they are an introvert or an extrovert. They more easily learn that others have different thoughts and feelings than they do. They want to interact and have friends at least some of the time depending on their level of being an introvert or an extrovert.

In order not to stand out, those at Level 4 tend to watch a lot, try to mimic, will laugh even if they don't understand what is funny, etc. Their goal is to blend in unless what they do differently is admired by others. Because they look normal and generally act normal, others demand that they be normal. When they miss social cues, their peers often don't understand what their problem is and give them a very hard time—especially teens.

Because they look pretty normal, no one may know they have difficulties until they hit the teen years when nuanced communication becomes the norm among their peers. They need help recognizing and understanding the shades of meaning that happen in nuanced communication. They need help to notice the small expressions or tones of voice that come before others are clearly mad, sad, glad, scared, etc. and what they mean. They often don't know what is going on inside them, or they struggle to put words to what they know, so they struggle to help others know them.

People in Level 4 will often have a lot of anxiety about missing social cues and struggle to be relaxed in any social situation. They can be a part of a group but don't necessarily feel like part of the group. They may struggle to define what is going on inside them at first, but as they become more proficient, they will relate more. They may feel lonely because no one understands what's really going on inside them. If they are really logical, they may understand they are different, but they may not have many feelings about it or care what others think or feel about them.

Levels of Inductive Reasoning Issues

Level 1 (L1) – High Impact They are so impacted that they don't have many, if any, verbal skills and need constant oversight and help.

Level 2 (L2) – Major Impact, Not Aware of Others or Themselves They don't really realize that others have different thoughts and feelings than they do until someone points it out to them. They are usually not aware of their own behavior, and others will need to point it out to them before they will look at it. And they will need a lot of help to know what they should do differently. They won't know what to do with that information and will need a lot of coaching to be socially appropriate. They will work at social skills because those in authority want them to or they think it is a rule, but it's very slow, repetitious learning.

Level 3 (L3) – Moderate Impact, Sometimes Aware of Others or Themselves Sometimes they know others have different thoughts and feelings than they do. Sometimes they are aware of their behavior. Sometimes they are totally unaware. They want to interact and have friends at least some of the time. They don't understand social rules or skills and miss a lot of the cues. They will work hard to learn to be socially appropriate and are personally motivated to work at it in order to have friends. Their level of motivation will depend on their level of being an introvert or an extrovert.

Level 4 (L4) – Minor Impact, Somewhat Aware of Others or Themselves These folks work very hard to appear normal. They get some of the body/social cues but miss some that are more nuanced. They struggle socially because their small missed cues stand out more because they appear so normal. This can cause them to be tentative or withdrawn in social situations, whether they are an introvert or an extrovert. They more easily learn that others have different thoughts and feelings than they do. They want to interact and have friends at least some of the time depending on their level of introvert or extrovert. They often think very differently from their peers. They often don't know what is going on inside them, or they struggle to put words to what they know, so they struggle to help others know them. Others often don't understand them, even when they explain themselves.

Introverts and Extroverts

We often forget that those with any kind of diagnosis still have character traits, including whether they are extroverts or introverts. *Extroverts generally gain energy by being around people and tend to process verbally with others* when they are trying to figure something out or deal with their feelings (often those with ADHD or bipolar). *Introverts are sucked dry energetically by being around others. They need time alone to process. Being alone rejuvenates them.* They have to go away and think by themselves to figure things out. If you try to talk with them, it just interrupts that process for them.

The level of impact, along with whether they are an extrovert or an introvert, will generally affect how soon they are diagnosed.

- **Level 2 Introverts** will play by themselves and never seek others to play with them. They won't know why they should interact with others. If someone shares their interest, they will talk about it. When they are done talking about their interest, they will leave, generally without any forewarning or care for the impact their behavior has on another. They often get diagnosed early in elementary school.
- **Level 2 Extroverts** will talk about their interest with anyone who is willing to listen. They will have no awareness of their impact on others, and they won't care. Adults will be amazed by a child's knowledge initially and put up with their talking far longer than peers. People will have to cut them off to shut them up and will be uncomfortable about having to do that, so they generally will avoid Level 2 Extroverts in the future if they can. They generally get diagnosed in preschool or early elementary.
- **Level 3 Introverts** will be very quiet and log everything they see. They will struggle to understand much about interacting with others and may be very happy just to play by themselves. They may become more anxious than others with IRI when around two or more people outside their family, but they won't know why they feel that way. And they will manage it by focusing on what they are interested in doing—by themselves. They may not get diagnosed until later in elementary school.
- **Level 3 Extroverts** will work hard at connecting and will struggle more to understand social cues. They are apparent even as young children because they lack much awareness about how their

behavior is impacting others. They will do things that frustrate or anger other children, and they will not understand why or what to do to repair relationships. In early years, peers will often forgive and forget for a time until they reach their limit and are no longer willing to play with them. Older children may bully them. They often get diagnosed early in elementary school.

- **Level 4 Introverts** will appear shy. They are often so quiet that others may not have a clue what is actually going on for them. They often don't know what is going on inside them, or they struggle to put words to what they know. They work hard to appear normal and not do things that bother others because they really don't want to stand out from others. Like extroverts, they will still struggle with some social cues and nuanced communication. They will often not repeat behavior that isn't accepted well. They often don't have a lot of motivation for making connections because they get so very tired working at it. They may have one or two longer-term friendships from early years. They may not get diagnosed until late teens or later in life. Or diagnosed with ADD, social phobia or social anxiety disorder.
- **Level 4 Extroverts** usually get diagnosed in later elementary or in teen years. Extroverts get diagnosed sooner than introverts because they want to connect with others more. In the beginning of a relationship or in a new situation, they may start out quiet because they are logging information and they don't want to appear different.

Again, being an introvert or an extrovert is on a continuum. High Introverts will not seek much interaction with others outside the requirements for school or a job. Low Introverts will need some time to themselves and will generally figure things out by themselves. Low Extroverts will tend to talk things out with someone, but they may not want a lot of time with others outside the family. High Extroverts will talk with lots of people, process with people and, depending on the level of IRI, do many to minimal social errors. The Myers-Briggs Type Indicator or the Keirsey Bates shortened version from the book, *Please Understand* Me, can help you determine whether you are an introvert or extrovert and how strongly you are one.

It's important for parents, partners, teachers, bosses, and clinicians to recognize whether the person with IRI is an introvert or extrovert and try to adjust their timing, demands, and expectations so those with IRI can be the most successful in their social interactions and in their work (school or job.) Extroverted parents often struggle more with introverted children. They can't understand how being around people can be draining when it's exciting and energizing for them. It's vitally important for them to accept that difference and accept that their child has IRI. They will struggle more openly with their grief. See the "Grief" section in Resources for more information.

Extroverts or Introverts

Extroverts generally gain energy by being around people. They tend to process verbally with others when they are trying to figure something out or deal with their feelings. *Introverts are sucked dry energetically by being around others.* They need time alone to process information. Being alone rejuvenates them. Adjust your expectations for those with IRI to meet their needs and have them be as successful as they can be.

Those with IRI need to plan for time alone or to not have too much time with others. You need to learn how to leave gracefully. Make sure you have enough "people time" or "alone time" to rejuvenate and to think.

Feelers and Thinkers

People fall into two categories of how they respond to the world. One is Feeling (the majority) and the other is Thinking. We gather information through our senses of seeing, hearing, touch, taste, and smell (and some would say a sixth sense of intuition, which requires inductive reasoning.) We then go either a Thinking route or Feeling route in our reaction or response to the information we have received.

Feelers will notice their feelings first. They may be mad, sad, glad, scared, confused, curious, etc. Once they have noticed their feelings, they will move to Thinking about their Feelings. They will make up a story about what happened and why. Their story will be based on their expectations or interpretations about what happened.

For example, we see someone we know walking down the side-walk towards us on the opposite side of the street. We wave, and we do not get a response. Feelers may immediately Feel upset in some way and wonder why the other person didn't respond. They will make up stories in their mind about why that happened based on their expectations or interpretations from past experiences. Here are some possibilities.

1. I feel sad or ashamed. He must not like me anymore if he doesn't respond.
2. I feel anxious or afraid. He must be mad at me. What am I going to do now?
3. I feel confused because I think he saw me, but I'm not really sure, so now I don't know what to do!
4. I feel angry that he didn't respond. What's his problem?
5. I feel worried because he must be so preoccupied that he didn't see me. He must have something awful going on.

There is a whole variety of feelings, and then thoughts, that can occur based on how we think of ourselves, how we think of the others involved, and what our past experiences with the same situation or the people involved have been.

Thinkers, on the other hand, will have lots of thoughts and may or may not get to their feelings. They may have some of the same thoughts as Feelers, but it may not occur to them to proceed to the feelings until they get more information about the situation. For example, if they think the person didn't see them, they may go through the following thoughts for more information:

1. I wonder why he didn't respond to my wave.
2. Did he see me or not?
3. What do I need to talk with him about?
4. How important is it?
5. Do I need to talk with him right now?
6. When will I see him next?
7. Will it be easier if I talk with him then?
8. If it is important for me to connect, should I wave again or cross the street and talk with him?
9. Should I just let it go for now and talk with him later at some point?

They may run through many thoughts quickly, or they may spend a great deal of time trying to figure out the answers to the questions they have. They will pursue the information from their thinking before they move to having their feelings. They have to come to some conclusion first. Then they will move to feeling mad, sad, glad, scared, confused, curious, etc. Some Thinkers are so involved with their thoughts that they don't recognize having any feelings and need to be coached to stop and figure their feelings out.

Once you have your feelings and thoughts you move on to needs or wants. Feelers will usually go to what they want first. No one wants to feel scared, sad, or mad, and so Feelers try to figure out what they can do to stop feeling that way. They will focus on a way to deal with their feelings by making a decision about:

1. What they want for themselves from the other person or
2. What they want to happen in that situation.

If you focus on what you can do to change the feelings you are having, you will be proactive about getting what you want. If you focus on what you want the other person to do, you turn your power over to the other person, and you may or may not get what you want.

Thinkers will usually focus on what they need first. They will think about the task they are to accomplish. They will decide what things they need to accomplish it. They will figure out what action they need to take to get the things they need to complete the task. They want all the information they think they need. Then they may look at wants—how they want to proceed, who they want to work with, what way they want to do the work, etc.

The single thing that is important to understand about those with IRI is that the odd behavior or socially inappropriate behavior is usually not based on feelings that they have towards the people they are around. Feeling-based people often interpret that others are responding out of what they are feeling just as they do. Most of those with IRI are responding out of their thinking. They may not have any feelings that they are aware of about you or the situation.

Feelers have to learn to hold their feelings and the thoughts they have about their feelings and find out what the person with IRI is meaning or intending. Otherwise they will react out of misinterpretation. The person with IRI won't understand what is going on and won't know how to respond. This can spiral into a lot of frustration or hurt that can be avoided.

Feelers and Thinkers

Feelers tend to react with feelings to whatever they experience before thinking about it. Thinkers tend to think about what they experience and may or may not move to their feelings.

If interacting with those with IRI, understand they are usually thinking a lot, and comments they make are often on the process and not about the other person. **The single thing that is important to understand about those with IRI is that the odd behavior or socially inappropriate behavior is usually not based on feelings that they have towards the people they are around.**

For those with IRI, understand that most people respond with feelings first. To have a good relationship with others, you may need to address others' feelings. And you may need to do that before you get your needs met. Also, most people who are Feelers do not understand Thinkers very well. You will have to explain yourself, or they won't understand you.

How to Use This Book and Worksheets

I recommend you read this book more than once. It is written in language that is specific enough for those with IRI to understand. It will help those of you who do not have IRI to begin to think and talk specifically in ways that are very beneficial to those who do have IRI. Fill out the worksheets at the end of the book for one person as you go through the information. If you have more than one family member that you think may have IRI, go through the book a second time to fill out worksheets for that second person. You may also want to fill out a form each year or half year if you see a lot of change, so you can track improvements and change the plan and focus of the work with the person who has IRI. Aspects will change over time and age.

The worksheets are designed to help you organize information that you figure out as you read through the book. It is a way to help you share information between those of you that have IRI and those that don't if both ready to talk about IRI. This book is not designed to help you resolve conflicts or frustrations, or past resentments and hurts. It is not meant to be used to make someone believe he has IRI. It is not meant to be used in anger or frustration ever. Please get help from a psychotherapist if those feelings keep occurring and aren't resolved. Please remember that those who have IRI usually are not trying to be hurtful. Because they have IRI, they don't understand how their thoughts or behavior will affect you.

Working with School Staff Using the Worksheets

In an ideal world, all staff and parents and a psychotherapist or other needed therapists would read this book and fill out the worksheets. They would talk together at an IEP meeting and make a plan for what aspects would be worked on at school, at home, and in therapy and how they would be worked on. Everyone would review things at the middle of the school year and again at the beginning of the next school year, with possible times in-between if something doesn't work or becomes a real problem.

In the real world, few schools and parents have the time and the financial means for all of that to happen. But do what you can and try to work with parents as much as possible. They have to work on some things at home while you work on some things at school if the student is going to succeed in the world.

Psychotherapists Using the Worksheets

In an ideal world, both parents and other involved family teens or adults at home would read this book. Each of you would fill out the worksheets, and all would meet to share and plan. You would talk about the aspects you each see, discuss how each of you would work on them with the child or teen with IRI, and set a priority on addressing the aspects. Parents or other adult family would trade off coming weekly with the child and discussing an aspect, the level, ways of how to work on it, and how that would help the child or teen. You all would agree on how you would help the child or teen and what the child or teen would do to help himself. Teens with IRI would read the book and fill out the form depending on the level of impact, age, focus, and motivation. With them, you might even be able to brainstorm ideas on how to work on an aspect. You would meet with parents, teens, or other adults every four to six months to review and make plans together. Again there's rarely the time and resources for all of this to happen.

In the real world, generally one parent can come and will be able to read the book and fill out the worksheets, especially if the child is not a teen yet. You and the parent should meet to review the worksheets, how aspects might be worked on, and determine a priority in discussing aspects with the child with IRI. I always have a parent present when I work with children who are not teens. It can be helpful to talk with the child present about one aspect at a time so he isn't overwhelmed. Discuss the level that you and the parent(s) think the child is at on that aspect and ask the child what he sees and experiences about that aspect. Share one to two examples. Talk about what each of you can do to work on it, explain the benefits of working on it, and get the child to agree to working on it. With teens, you may want to have them read the book and fill out the form depending on the level of impact, age, focus, and motivation. I've shared how I split the time working with teens in Doing Psychotherapy or Counseling. I find the more the child understands the issue, what can be done, and how working on it will help him, the more motivated he is to work on it.

Couples/Partners Using the Worksheets

If you have a relatively positive relationship without a lot of conflict, you can meet as a couple on your own to share your worksheets. It helps to agree on a specific time each week for no longer than an hour, as that lowers the stress for those with IRI. Discuss only one aspect per meeting so that the person with IRI is not overwhelmed. Share the level of the aspect and talk about one to two examples. The person with IRI should share his thinking attached to the behavior so the partner can begin to understand how the one with IRI thinks. The partner should listen and share what she understand her partner is saying. Once you have agreement that the person with IRI is understood, then the partner without IRI should share her thoughts until she is understood and then her feelings about the example. This is information only sharing. If you have the history and tools to resolve the different viewpoints and experiences and plan for how things will be handled in the future, then do so. Otherwise, it is best to work with a psychotherapist to resolve things. I recommend seeing a marriage and family therapist because they are trained in the dynamics and patterns of relationships, as well as counseling skills. It's best if the therapist reads this book before working with you, or they will not understand the partner with IRI.

If you have a lot of conflict in the relationship, please only use the worksheets individually unless you see a psychotherapist. Going over the same conflict on your own will often increase the pain, frustration, and self-protection that can destroy your relationship. Partners of those with IRI need more support outside the relationship because of the lack of empathy from their partner. Extra time for them with their friends can be very beneficial.

Working with Families Using the Worksheets

I recommend that families work with a psychotherapist in order to keep conversation focused, keep to only one aspect, and get help with family patterns, as well as resolving conflict. I work with various members in different combinations over time depending on the age, the aspects, and the level of conflicts. Often when the person with IRI gets better, siblings will want to retaliate for what they have endured so far. It's best to work with them individually to resolve their grief and pain.

Whom to Share the Worksheets With

When you are done, you can share the worksheets with those who are ready to talk about it. This could be parents sharing with each other, a couple where one has IRI, a teacher and parent of a student with IRI, a psychotherapist and parent(s) or other family members where one has IRI, or a psychotherapist and client who has IRI.

Once worksheets are filled out, plan a time to sit down regularly and share your worksheets. I recommend talking about only one aspect at a time if you are sharing with a person with IRI so you don't overwhelm him. Often doing this with a neutral third party, like a psychotherapist, is extremely helpful.

If there are past hurts among family members, it's important for each person to be able to talk about his or her thinking, feeling, and experiences around that aspect in a place where he or she feels safe. These worksheets will not guide you on resolving them, so get help from a professional who knows how to help you. Don't use it to hurt one another more or make someone believe what you believe. This is designed to share information only for those who are ready to hear it. Or it is for you, as an individual, to get at least one idea on how to work with an aspect, whether it is yours or another family member's. There are many tools already developed to help you work on an aspect as long as you understand what you need help with. The resources section has many tools listed.

Filling out the Worksheets at the End of the Book

Now that you have some understanding of levels, extroverts and introverts, Feelers and Thinkers, go to the back of the book and copy the worksheets. Fill out your best guess on the overall level, introvert vs. extrovert, and Feeler vs. Thinker continuums. As you read the aspects, write down the level that you think applies to that aspect for you or the person in your life who you think has inductive reasoning issues. Give one to two examples of what you have seen that supports your best guess.

Chapter 2 | Understanding Aspects of Inductive Reasoning Issues

It's estimated our brain has a billion neurons and each neuron has thousands of connections to other neurons. Everyone is wired differently based on his or her life experiences and genetic makeup. Everyone will have a different set of aspects and a different level of difficulty with each of those aspects. You will find some things that fit in this list and others that don't fit at all. Some aspects will fit all the time, and others will show up only in certain situations. Few people will have all these aspects. It will depend on how the brain has organized itself. Even those who do not have IRI can have some of these aspects. But they can recognize when they have impacted a relationship negatively, have empathy, and correct the behavior more easily.

It will be important to view the person you think has IRI in a variety of situations. The individual usually knows how to respond at home because he or she has been trained by the family rules and responses and will feel most comfortable acting out at home. But out in the world, the rules are different, and the one with IRI has to figure them out. You will see different aspects at school, in the park, at the store, at Girl or Boy Scouts, at church, in karate, etc. then you will at home. Be sure to be able to watch the person in a variety of settings with peers, teachers, bosses, and strangers to get the best idea of what aspects he or she may be struggling with.

I hope you find it helpful to sort out which of the following aspects you or another may have and gain some resources that help you. I hope this information helps you set appropriate expectations that encourage those who have IRI to be as successful as they can be and results in less frustration for everyone.

Eye Contact

Many people on the spectrum of IRI have been given the diagnosis of social phobia or social anxiety disorder often due to lack of eye contact, lack of interaction, and avoidance of groups of people. The wish of those with IRI not to be in crowds or out in the world generally has little to do with being afraid of people due to a traumatic incident—which is what occurs for most people who have a social phobia. I think those with IRI often lack filters and feel overwhelmed.

For example, I have had a fear of talking in front of groups most of my life, and it goes back to a childhood incident that I've been working through. I had to understand what happened to me and why I responded with fear. I had to clear the autonomic nervous system response of fear to the triggers that happened back then before I could relax. I've gotten to a place where I only get a bit nervous during the five minutes or so before I have to talk. So my experience created an emotional response that led to the fear of being in front of a group (the most common fear among people).

For those with IRI, it can be a different experience totally. It often does not have to do with being afraid because of a particular experience they had with a group of people. *Those with IRI often are overwhelmed in any group by the amount of information they are managing.* They can't get over their need to *consciously* log, correlate, and determine the meaning of what they are seeing. And the information gets more nuanced as people get older, so it makes it more difficult to know what meaning to make out of what they are seeing, hearing, etc. They can learn to cope in a variety of ways with the anxiety that groups cause for them. Those that are extroverts by nature will have an easier time than those that are introverts.

I think this is why those with IRI often don't look people in the face. They try to limit the information intake. There are far more things to log visually than with any other sense. And it may be difficult to sort information from both the visual and the auditory at the same time, especially if they have filter issues. They may need to limit visual information so they can take in the verbal cues and know what they are required to do, especially directions from an authority figure.

Another aspect may be that if they see a person or an interaction, then they are responsible for understanding and knowing about it and interacting about it. And it may take them some time to determine what happened and why, especially L3s and possibly L4s. So they can be several seconds behind in understanding and in their response, which can make them stand out, appear odd, and/or make them self-conscious. They may also need some time to understand what they have logged in a situation and need some down time to figure it out without taking in any more information. A feeling-oriented person often assumes these people with IRI have poor self-esteem. They may struggle with self-esteem, but it's just as likely they are limiting the information they take in.

Another possible explanation for lack of eye contact is they may not have a sense of personal boundaries the way those who can do inductive reasoning do. So when they look in another's eyes, they feel as if they lose their sense of self. That also is a very overwhelming sensation and one we all would avoid. So of course they wouldn't look you in the eye.

How many of us, who can do inductive reasoning look away when we are thinking things through? I know I do it, and I see most people do it. But I return to look at the person in front of me periodically as I am talking. Those who have IRI may need to be coached to do that in order to fit in. If they have already learned to look people in the eye, they may hold it non-stop, which can be uncomfortable for the other person. They may look like the deer in the headlights with eyes a little too open but not really present. Working with a mirror and trying to copy typical behavior with a coach can be helpful to fitting in.

They may develop a social phobia after a while of missing social cues and being ridiculed because of it. Family and therapists have to really understand what's going on when those with IRI are afraid. We have to ask the right questions in order to plan the appropriate help. Do they feel overwhelmed when around others? Does not looking at someone help them to listen? Do they think they have to respond if they make eye contact? Do they know how to respond when they make eye contact? Are they fearful they will miss social cues because they have in the past? Are they afraid of being ridiculed? And then we have to find ways to help them deal with eye contact. It may be explaining something about their struggle with some people. You will need to help them know which people to share with and which people with whom they shouldn't share. They may need to practice looking at others periodically and know how often or where to look when they aren't looking at them. You have to help them find the things they need to do so they are the most successful they can be out in the world.

Eye Contact

To understand those with IRI, their lack of eye contact can be:

- A way to limit information in order to follow directions
- A way to limit information in order to think and not be distracted
- Due to feeling overwhelmed by others
- Due to feeling overwhelmed by the amount of information coming in
- Due to anxiety
- Due to a fear based on social difficulties in the past
- Feeling shy or embarrassed
- A way to set a personal boundary

Don't make assumptions that the same thing is true each time. Ask to find out the difficulty and what support you can give.

For those with IRI, here are some tips about eye contact.

- Learn at least to glance at others as you are talking with them. They need the contact to feel connected to your conversation. It also gives you a way to see if they are still listening to you or if their eyes are focused elsewhere. Then you need to stop or check in with them to see if they are still interested or listening.
- Learn to look others in the eye when you are first meeting them. It tells them you are confident about yourself. This will likely reduce bullying in school and can impress a teacher, supervisor, or boss.
- Let others know you are thinking and ask them to give you a minute if it takes you longer to figure something out. Otherwise, people won't know how to interpret the pause and may decide any number of reasons for your quietness, all of which may be inaccurate.
- Let others know you are managing anxiety or fear and you will respond in a moment. This is good to share in families, but be careful in public with this information. It can increase bullying or reduce others' confidence in your abilities. Talk with a parent or therapist about when and where to do this.

When people understand one another, there is much more compassion and tolerance than when they don't know what is happening or why it is happening. So the more information we can share in appropriate ways with the appropriate people, the more chance there is for good communication and good relationships to develop.

Body Language of Others

Most of us see/hear a group of body cues for a person (facial expression, body movements, how he or she holds the body, and/or tones in the voice), and we make the inductive leap of defining that group of body cues with a single meaning—mad, sad, glad, scared, funny, strange, etc. We attach a level of importance to the meaning about it that allows us to store and recover it easily. And we do it without consciously thinking through it. It happens for us in a moment or two.

Those with IRI can't easily make meaning out of what they see, hear, touch, taste, and smell. So, they have to look around and consciously log each person's response, look into that person's file to see what matches (if anything), or figure out now what each person is feeling, wanting, or saying. They will not sense what the other person is feeling at all. They have to figure it out consciously. This can take time and slow their response.

Those with IRI are often out of sync and can't understand how their reactions and behavior don't match the mood of the room or group of people they are around. They may not know to take the time to understand what is happening before they try to interact. They may not be able to understand what is happening in the group before interacting. Or they may not even think about others at all. Coaching those with IRI to understand the need to figure out what is happening in a group before speaking up and practicing what behavior will help them successfully join a group is vital to being successful in the world. There are many books available to help with social skills. Psychotherapists trained in social skills training, social skills groups, and speech therapists at school can all be helpful.

Body Language

To help those with IRI, understand they struggle to read both others' body cues as well as their own. Give them *specific* information about how to read others' body, especially facial, cues. Telling them *specifically* what they are doing facially or with their body, or things they are saying, how others will experience what they are saying, and what they need to do or say differently is important for them to learn to be socially appropriate.

For those with IRI, find people who will give you the information you need. Find at least one friend who will help you by answering questions you have about why people reacted the way they did. Ask your parents every day the questions you have about other's behaviors. Keep a little notebook for listing questions because it will be hard to remember them later. Find friends or a partner as you grow older who is willing to accept you and be helpful by answering these questions. See a therapist that knows how to help with social skills any time in your life.

Body Awareness of Self

The flip side of not being able to read another's body cues is that those with IRI often can't read their own body cues either. They may not be paying attention to what they are feeling or experiencing because they are working so hard at figuring out others or the situation. Or they may have a hard time hearing themselves, just as they have a hard time hearing another. They may use a tone of voice that is not appropriate to the situation or is very monotone. They may talk very loudly because they can't hear themselves well. They may talk loudly because they are hearing everything in the room coming in at the same volume level, and they have to talk over all the sounds they are hearing in their head at one time. See "Sensory Overload or Lack of Filters" in "Sensory Issues" in this chapter for more information.

Whatever they are feeling may come out in their tone of voice or facial expression without their being aware of it. Most of us as we grow up learn the social skill to hide how we feel until it is right or safe to share our feelings. But those with IRI may not be able to identify what they are feeling, and/or they may not be able to tell how they are expressing themselves. For instance, their body may not be facing the one to whom they are talking. They may be looking at someone else or somewhere else when they are trying to talk to a person in front of them. Or they may say something very logical that is totally not appropriate to the situation or feelings of another person with them (L2, L3.) They have to learn how they are coming across to others from someone they can trust. It's important for those with IRI to learn to pay attention to their body in their interactions with others and how to be socially appropriate. A therapist can help parents learn how to teach their child. The therapist can work with those who have IRI to teach them to notice and be appropriate in their interactions. Small social skill groups are also really helpful.

Those with IRI may have a brain/body disconnect due to a possible variety of factors, including what happened pre- and pari-natally (in the womb, through birth, and the first year of life), toxicity exposure, genetics, brain trauma, etc. They will have to practice physical things more before their body easily does it, and some things may never come easily. Modalities like educational kinesiology, sensory integration, and energy medicine can help. Seeing a naturopath who knows how to clear chemicals from toxic exposure or heavy metals can help. (See "Resources.")

Body tension is a cue for us to stop and figure out what is going on and how we need to respond. When we feel threatened, our body goes into the fight-or-flight mode. We get ready to fight what may be after us, or we get ready to flee from it. This is a very primitive response system in our body. If we aren't aware of our body, we won't get the message we need in order to address the threat. Since those with IRI are often overwhelmed by information, their body may be in the fight-or-flight mode most of the time. If you have IRI, it's vitally important to learn to deal with the stress of that. (See "Stress, Worry, Fear, Anxiety, and Panic" on page 98.) You may need to leave a social situation because you are on overload. You may need to plan down time in order to relate well with your family or friends. Learn to check in with your body to see how you feel and whether you need to do something different.

See a therapist to help you become more aware of your feelings and to learn to plan for managing anxiety and learn the many ways you can relax your body. The Resource Section lists various therapies and the way in which they can help with different aspects of IRI.

Improving Body Awareness and Increasing Relaxation

You will find that teens will often avoid these suggestions. If you can start when they are little, they will continue to seek and use the following methods that work for them. If you are using this with an older child who resists, you can always offer them periodically to see when he or she is mature enough to accept something.

Massage

Massage can be a really helpful way to focus on one's body. Parents can massage hands and feet in order to have a nice non-verbal connection with children and teens. Partners can do it with each other. There are books on massage that you can get and follow. You can massage your own feet, hands, head, etc. Getting a massage from a massage therapist who will work each part of the body can be helpful.

To give a hand massage to someone else, hold the other person's hand in your hands. Begin by using your thumbs to stroke from the center of the palm out to the sides. Massage the sides of the fingers (not the top or bottom) from the base of the finger out to the tip. Sweep your fingertips up and down the back of the hand between the bones of the fingers. This hand massage will stimulate the six energy meridians that run through the hands and help energy to flow more fully and clearly in the body. It can help release over-energy in the body (anxiety) as well. Use the same techniques on the feet.

Pons Tapping or Squeezing

A way to feel your body more is to tap or squeeze each part of your body. Use a cupped hand to tap over your whole body except for the private parts (genital area) to increase your awareness of how your body feels. You want a strong enough tap or squeeze to feel it without any pain attached. This stimulates the pons area of the brain and helps to make more brain/body connections. You can do this for yourself or get a family, close friend, or massage therapist to do it.

Pillow Wrestling

Pillow wrestling works really well for elementary-age children and below. The parent and child kneel facing each other with each holding a pillow by its sides. Place the pillow faces together. Say, 'Go.' Have the child push from the belly and try to push you over with his or her pillow. Give in at times and win at times. This will help children to be more in touch with their body at their core. You can use it when they are angry at you or others or afraid because something happened that scared them. It helps them get the energy out without being destructive when angry or withdrawn when scared.

Yoga

Yoga is a helpful way to relax and be more in touch with your body. The stretching and holding postures help you become more aware of your body, especially if the instructor is good at directing you to pay attention to different parts of your body through the session. Breathing forms can also help relax and oxygenate your body and brain.

Breathing

Learning to breathe deeply can be helpful in relieving stress and oxygenating your body and brain. Taking a deep breath in through your nose while counting to four, pausing, and then exhaling out your mouth for a count of eight can help you relax your body. The *Relaxation and Stress Reduction Workbook* is outstanding and has many helpful exercises.

Checking in with Your Body

Teaching people with IRI to stop and to check in with their body can be really helpful. Don't we all need to do that regularly for our well-being? There are times that are natural for most of us to do this—waking, going to sleep, before and after eating (this helps us know the sensation of when our body is hungry or full), before making a transition from one activity to another, and after making a transition from one activity to another. Transitions are often difficult to manage for those with IRI, so recognizing what it feels like when you are feeling stressed can help you know what you need to do for your anxiety/stress. (See the section "Stress, Worry, Fear, Anxiety, and Panic" under "Feelings" section in this chapter.) Checking in after a transition can help you learn that you made it through a transition just fine, but you may still need to do some calming techniques. Otherwise you might not note that it went well and just remember it being difficult to make the transition.

If you are helping those with IRI, you may have to teach them how to check in with their body first. Have them feel each part of their body by directing them to notice what they are feeling on their head, face, neck, shoulders, upper arms, elbows, lower arms, wrists, hands, fingers, chest, back, abdomen, hips, buttocks, groin, thighs, knees, calves, ankles, feet, and toes. You can start this by age two as they learn their body parts. There are many DVDs showing how to do this for the general population which can also be helpful to those with IRI.

There are resources available to help with sensory connections or overload. Sensory integration therapy, Brain Gym/

educational kinesiology, cranial-sacral work, visceral manipulation and structural integration (with a gentle practitioner), energy medicine, and working with an occupational therapist who does sensory integration can all help. See the section "Sensory Issues" in this chapter or "Resources" for more information and for books.

Body Awareness

Our body gives us information about whether we are safe (flight-or-fight response), whether our boundaries have been crossed (tension or angry feelings), whether things are going well (relaxed or happy), etc. Learning to listen to our body is vital for us to have the information we need to survive and to thrive in the world.

To help those with IRI, teach them about how to tune into their body, what various body tensions mean, how they can relieve tension, what boundaries are for, and how to set and maintain them well, etc. Massage, pons tapping or squeezing, pillow wrestling, yoga, breathing and learning to check in with and relax their body can help them cope. Other modalities, like sensory integration therapy, Brain Gym-education kinesiology, cranial-sacral work, visceral manipulation and structural integration (with a gentle practitioner), and energy medicine, can all help to change the connection they have to their body system more permanently.

For those with IRI, develop a routine to take time to check in with your body. Let your body teach you when you need to change something. Learn ways to help your body relax. Get help if you can't relax your body. You don't have to stay in worry, tension, anxiety, or fear. You can learn ways to do things differently and ways to think that will help you be more relaxed and happier.

Making Meaning

When you ask someone with IRI a question, the answer you will often get is one that is very literal or logical. Here's an example.

You ask, "What does it mean *when they say* it was the stick that broke the camel's back?" Because this is a very broad and general question, those with IRI will struggle to give an answer. They will struggle to find the right file. They don't know who "they" are so they can't access a person file. They have no personal experience with a camel, so there's no file or a limited one for that. They generally have a "stick" file, so they will go there to look. If they do respond to the question, it won't be in the way those who can do inductive reasoning would respond. They might think it was a very big stick or a very hard stick or a stick that was swung so hard that it broke the camel's back. They have no experience with how a camel carries things. They will think the stick broke the camel's back because that's what the question says happened. They won't understand that there were many sticks in a pack already on the camel's back and this last one made it too heavy for the camel to carry. If they are smart or older, they will look up the exact meaning of that phrase on the Internet and respond more appropriately.

If you ask, "What does it mean *when the author says* it was the stick that broke the camel's back?" those with IRI will think something along the lines of "I don't know the author; you better ask him." They aren't being smart-mouthed; they are being literal. They don't know the author, so they don't know how the author thinks. They won't be able to do the inductive reasoning that allows them to generalize an answer based on what they know or what others have said about a stick breaking the camel's back or about the general meaning of that phrase. They will only think about that author because that's what you asked about.

If you ask "What do *you think it means* when the author says it was the stick that broke the camel's back?" you will get a very different view of the world because those with IRI don't experience the world the same way most people do. And it won't be wrong; it will be what they experience because you asked them what they thought.

So, you may get very different answers based on the *exact question* you ask and the level of knowledge those with IRI have about the topic. The more specific a question that you ask, the more specific and accurate an answer you will get. They won't broaden the question because they struggle to do the inductive reasoning that requires that. They hear exactly what you say or read exactly what you write and will attempt to respond to exactly what you ask.

It's important for those of us who can do inductive reasoning to learn to ask a question that is specific to the information we want to receive. This is actually great training for being a very good communicator. And we Feelers have to learn to hold our feelings and check our interpretations or conclusions before we react. That is actually very respectful.

Making Meaning

If you are communicating with someone with IRI, remember the specific words you use will impact the information you get from that person. Once you have a question in mind, learn to think about what information you really need or want and then adapt the question to be specific so that it will access the information that you are really seeking. Those with IRI will need to be patient with you as you do this process. You may have to ask for a moment to figure out what you are asking for or requesting.

For those with IRI, here's a process to make sure that what you think others are asking from you is in fact what they are asking. We all misinterpret, so all you are doing is clarifying information.

- Identify in your mind what you think others are asking.
- Ask if you can verify your thinking.
- Tell them what you think they are asking for.
- Ask them if that is correct or if they need to clarify anything.

> Once they have finished clarifying and said yes to what you think they are asking, then proceed to respond to the question or request as it fits for you. Just because you understand what they are asking for does not mean you have to do it. You now have a choice to say yes or no based on correct information.

Translating Meaning to Other Situations or Other Environments

Most of us will learn from one situation and translate that learning to other situations that are similar. You can't assume that those with IRI will assign the same meaning they have learned about one situation to any other similar situation or from one person to another who is similar because they won't note the similarity unless they are taught to do that specifically.

For example, if you say you love chocolate and really want some for Valentine's Day, those with IRI will probably buy you the chocolate they like or any chocolate that is the first they see that appeals to them. Unless you say you want or like a specific brand, they probably won't get it for you. And the reverse is true. If you tell them you want a particular chocolate, then those with IRI will go out of their way to get that chocolate, even if they have to order it and can't get it by Valentine's Day. Or, they may not get you any if they can't find that specific brand. So it's important to understand that they put the time and care into trying to find it and they couldn't find it. It's not that they didn't care about you if they don't get it. But you may have to ask if they tried because they may not think to tell you that they tried to find it.

When those with IRI don't assign the same meaning to similar things, they won't think to buy you chocolates for any other holiday or event. But they may buy the same thing every year for Valentine's Day until you tell them you want something else. It doesn't mean they don't care. If they didn't care, they would do nothing. They are choosing to do what you said you wanted or liked because they care about you. They have no need for new things, new situations, or new routines because it requires additional processing from them. Every situation or person is new and has to be figured out each time. So, they will choose the same thing until they know you want something else.

Giving them several options often doesn't work well either. If you give them a list, they may try to get them all or give up in frustration at being forced to choose one or some. Or if you say, "Surprise me," it may be too overwhelming for them to choose at all, or they will just choose the first one on the list to reduce their stress. A choice between two may work, and then you get somewhat of a surprise since you don't know which one. It's not that they don't care; they just struggle with inductive reasoning and being on information overload most of the day.

It's important to understand that the information stays specific to you and whatever you have talked about. They don't necessarily relate it to other situations or with other people. Unless they are taught a rule that most people like chocolates for Valentine's Day, they won't understand that. They are very literal and will keep that information attached to you alone. Even if two or three others say they like chocolates for Valentine's Day, the person with IRI will log that info for them as individuals. They may not make the larger assumption that most people like chocolates for Valentine's Day, even though stores are filled with heart-shaped chocolates that time of year.

And this is true for any topic for them. It can be very difficult when your child or partner does not translate learning from one situation to another. The person with IRI often appears not to have learned anything from an experience because you don't see the person with IRI using that information in a new but similar experience. You will have to teach the person with IRI to translate the learning from one situation to another that is similar. You can coach them to think of similar past experiences and what worked and didn't work. Talk about how the past choices might work or not work in the new situation. And brainstorm other possible choices for the new situation.

Translating Meaning

Everyone interprets things differently. Those with IRI will struggle to translate meaning or learning from one situation to another.

When working with those with IRI, we need to be specific in our communication and requests. We need to teach them to think about a similar situation, to note what worked or didn't work before, and to think what they could try to do now that might work. We need to teach them to ask questions of parents, teachers, and maybe a few peers to find out what people mean and what they expect of one with IRI. We need to own our interpretations, assumptions, and expectations and have appropriate expectations of those with IRI. We need to recognize the caring they are already doing. We need to help them to expand their caring towards their self, us, and others.

For those with IRI, you need to understand that everyone thinks differently and not like you. You need to be specific in your communication and requests. You need to recognize that you have your own interpretations, assumptions, and expectations. You need to learn to share them with people who are important to you. You need to be patient when others don't understand you and be willing to explain yourself. Others are caring enough to ask questions about you because they want to understand and relate with you. They are taking their time to ask about you. You need to meet them halfway and take your time to explain yourself to them. Then you need to learn ways to ask about them that improve the relationship between the two of you. Get coaching from a psychotherapist if you struggle with this.

Grouping Similar Things

Those with IRI don't automatically group similar things. A person who is mad may have facial features that look the same as another person who is mad, but those with IRI won't note that. A person who is puzzled can look very similar when mad or look similar to someone else who is mad. Those with IRI don't group similar expressions into one meaning. So they have to figure out each person *individually, in a detailed way, each time.* They have to figure out each situation each time, even if they have been there before because today is different.

This can be exhausting for family and teachers. It's just as exhausting to those with IRI. Using different types of rules can help those with IRI. (See the section "Mega-rules, Rules, and Sub-rules" on page 88.) Having those with IRI get training to read facial and body cues can help. There are games for this you can play at home together, and there are videos and apps they can play individually. You can also work with an occupational therapist, counselor, speech therapist, or psychotherapist to practice reading facial expressions.

Grouping Similar Things

To help those with IRI, understand they generally don't group similar things or attach old meanings to new things that are similar. It can help to point out similarities between things. It can help to share social rules that apply. These individuals may need help to shift an old belief because the other person or the situation has changed. Teach them that rules change each year. They also change depending on the type of relationship they are dealing with (peer, adult, teacher, boss, etc.)

For those with IRI, learn to listen to those who are trying to help you understand social interaction. Work on using mega-rules, rules, and sub-rules (see the section "Mega-rules, Rules, and Sub-rules" on page 88) to help organize information so you can find more easily what you need to do in various situations.

Empathy

Empathy is the action of understanding, being aware of, being
sensitive to, and experiencing
the feelings,
thoughts,
and experience
of other people
without being in their situation yourself
and without them telling you directly what they are experiencing.

If you have IRI, you may feel rather overwhelmed just by reading that. Or you may feel pretty lost or confused. Or you may think you can easily do some of it but not all of it. You can learn to do this over time to some extent with those you are very close to.

When we try to understand another person, we first think about our own experiences that are similar to what the other person is currently experiencing. We draw information about how to treat the other person based on how we were treated or how we wanted to be treated. If we don't have a common experience, we then imagine our self in the place of the other person to feel what it would feel like to be in that situation. We pay attention to how we would want to be treated. Then we try to treat the other person that way. We all get it right many times, partially right sometimes, and totally wrong once in a while. Learning to ask what the other person needs or wants can be very helpful. Offer what you think you would like to the other person to see if he or she would like that or not. Or ask if the person would like something else.

People with IRI can come across as emotionally ignorant people because they can't do empathy well or at all. They struggle to make meaning out of what they see, hear, touch, taste, or smell, so they often don't have the time to try to imagine someone else's point of view. Or else they don't know how to do it. If L3s or L4s have had a similar experience, they can be very caring in their response, but often it is sympathy, not empathy.

Sympathy is when you express your feelings about a situation *you* had that is similar to the other person's situation. This can be using some inductive reasoning. But the same person may not be able to imagine a situation where he or she has not had a similar experience.

This can be confusing for others because those with IRI seem empathic at times and totally oblivious at other times, so people don't know what to expect from them.

It can help to teach those with IRI to say a few sentences, instead of being totally quiet, like:

1. I hear you.
2. Wow!
3. Hmm.
4. Oh.
5. That must be hard (if the person cries).

Or they can learn to ask what the other person needs right now. Then they can respond to that need even if they don't understand fully what the other person is experiencing. This way they can still show caring even if they can't show empathy.

Empathy

Empathy is the action of understanding, being aware of, being sensitive to, and experiencing
the feelings,
thoughts,
and experience
of other people
without being in their situation yourself
and without them telling you directly what they are experiencing.

Empathy does not mean care. One can have empathy, shut it off, and do very uncaring acts. Or people may be unable to take caring action because they feel too much empathy and are frozen or have to run away not to be overwhelmed. And one can struggle with empathy but be very caring. *Understand that those with IRI often can't do empathy very well or at all, but they are often very caring at times to people who are important to them.*

Sympathy is when you express your feelings about a situation that happened to you that is similar to the other person's. This can be confusing for others because those with IRI seem empathic at times and totally oblivious at other times

For those with IRI, learning to ask what the other person needs or wants can be very helpful. Offer what you think you would like to the other person to see if he or she would like that or not. Or ask if the person would like something else.

Understanding and Caring about Others

If you are interacting with those with IRI, it's important to clearly state the meaning for them. You have to share not only that you are happy but also why you are happy, or those with IRI won't make the connection between those pieces of information. This can be frustrating for the parent, child, teacher, partner, or boss. You can get very tired of explaining each and every thing. But people with IRI often can't make those connections, and they have no control over that. They often act uncaring because they don't understand or don't know what to do. Their brains can't do the inductive reasoning, so they log only one way to think about something. But they can learn multiple ways of thinking if you teach them. They can learn the process of empathy and practice it. And once they know something about you, they generally will never forget it. It is always in the file they carry in their head about you.

When they care about you, they can put a tremendous amount of work into understanding you. *They can be very caring and solicitous if they know what you need or want.* It is important to clearly tell those with IRI what you need and why or what you want/like and why. This helps them to understand you since they can't read the body cues well. Dropping hints will not work. Nor will giving them a look.

Most of us, including those with IRI, want others to understand us. But often we don't clearly state what we think, feel, want, or need or the reason why. We often just react. In order for those with IRI to understand us, we have to *practice sharing all the information*—what we saw/heard/felt physically, what we thought about/how we interpreted what we sensed or felt, what we felt emotionally, and what we want or what we need now. The more you can do that, the easier it is for people with IRI to understand and respond appropriately. Once they understand, they can work to be careful about what they say or how they say it. But you have to be direct and clear and state what most of us would consider obvious because their brains can't do inductive reasoning well.

One older man did many physical things for his daughter like help build a garden bed. But the way in which he said things was often discounting or demeaning, which is what he had learned from his father. He had to be willing to listen to what she said, be willing learn to say things differently, and continue to work on saying things differently in order to heal that relationship. She had to be patient in telling him what was meaningful to her and why. And she had to be patient with the amount of time it took him to learn.

Understanding and Caring about Others

If you are communicating with those with IRI, it's important to clearly state the meaning for them. You have to share not only that you are happy but also why you are happy, or those with IRI won't make the connection between those pieces of information.

For those with IRI, it is important to learn to express caring in ways that have meaning for the other person, which may be different than for you, even if you don't understand it. You will have to learn to ask if others feel cared about. You will need to ask what you can do or say so that those who are important to you feel cared about. And you will need to work on what and how and when you say things in order to be caring and have what you say received as caring. We all work on this in relationships.

Their Impact on Others

Those with IRI often can't tell what their impact is on others. A person may get angry with them or misunderstand them, and they will not understand why. They think they have been clear in what they have said. But often they are on a different topic or say things in a way that offends others. They often don't realize that others think differently than they do. Once they understand that others think differently than they do, they often don't know how to go about communicating with someone who thinks differently. It's like being in a foreign country speaking a different language. You often don't know exactly how to word things or what the common meanings (idioms) are for things. You make many mistakes as you attempt to learn them.

It is important to tell those with IRI how their behavior is impacting you and how most people will interpret their behavior and what their response will be. You need to give them a string of information. Here is a string of sentences with blanks to help you share all the information that those with IRI need.

1. When you did or said ______________________________,
   Name the specific behavior they did or thing they said and how they said it using descriptive words. Use the exact words they said and exactly how they said the words—loud, soft, mumbled, etc.—and not your interpretation of it.
2. I thought ______________________________________.
   Give them your interpretation here, such as "you were upset" or "you didn't care."

3. That made me feel ______________________________.
   Use words such as mad, sad, glad, scared, puzzled, uncomfortable, etc.

4. And that leads me to want to do ______________________.
   Say the behavior you feel want to do, which may be to talk with them about their behavior, give them a consequence, ignore them, etc.

5. Most people would think ___________________________.
   Tell them how you think most people would interpret their behavior or words, which may not be how you interpret it.

6. Most people would feel ______________________________.
   Use words such as mad, sad, glad, scared, confused, bored, etc. Share what you think most people would feel, especially if you interpreted it differently and felt differently from you think most people would.

7. And others would most likely ______________________.
   Use your best guess at what actions others would take.

8. If you don't want others to ____________ [*name the action*], you need to change your behavior, ____________________ __________. *Say the specifics of their behavior you listed above, in number 1.*

9. You might consider doing this instead: _________________.
   Give them two or three ideas about behavior or words they could use instead.

10. Most people would think ____________________________.
    Say how you think most people would interpret those new behaviors.

11. Most people would feel ______________________________.
    Tell how you think most people would feel about those new behaviors.

12. And others would most likely ___________________________.
    Use your best guess at what others would do in response to those new behaviors.

Here's a specific example. Your child walks out of the room without telling anyone anything. You need to call him back or go out and talk with him if people are still there and share the following information:

1. When you walked out of the room without telling anyone anything,
2. I thought that was odd and I wondered where you were going.
3. I felt confused because I didn't know how to interpret your behavior. And I felt concerned because I didn't know if you were having a problem or where you were going.
4. That leads me to want to set aside a time to talk with you about your behavior so others don't feel left suddenly or get upset at you and so you will know what to do in the future to avoid others misunderstanding you.
5. Most people would think that was odd behavior and wonder what they had done to cause you to leave. Or they would think it was very rude to be left that way without any explanation.
6. Most people would feel uncomfortable, and they wouldn't know how to respond to that behavior. It would stay in their mind on some level until they understood what was going on. Or they would be angry at being left without an explanation of where you were going and why.
7. And others would most likely tend to avoid you or be angry with you in the future until they understood what you were thinking and doing.

8. If you don't want others to feel uncomfortable or angry or avoid you in the future, you need to change your behavior. It is important not to walk out of the room without telling others why you are leaving.
9. You might say one of these things. Excuse me. I need to use the restroom. I forgot something and I'm going to go get it. I have become pretty tired and need to lie down, etc.
10. Then most people would think you have a good reason to leave, understand why you are leaving, and not be concerned.
11. Most people would then feel very comfortable.
12. And others would most likely want to be around you in the future.

This is how specific you need to be when people have IRI. They think differently and draw different conclusions from those who can do inductive reasoning.

You also have to learn to ask specific questions if you want to understand what they were thinking when they chose their behavior. Here's an example of some questions you might ask in the same situation.

1. When I saw you leaving, I wondered what you were thinking. Will you tell me what you were thinking then? (And follow their thinking to their conclusions.)
2. What were you feeling then?
3. What did you need or want then?
4. Are there other ways to get what you need or want without walking out and not telling anyone anything?
5. Did you think about how your behavior would impact other people?
6. Do you think it's important to think about that?

7. Are you willing to hear what I think others thought or felt at the time? (If they are willing, then share the information from the prior list.)
8. Is that what you want others to think about you or feel towards you?
9. Are you willing to change your behavior?
10. What do you think you can do differently next time? (If they can't come up with something, offer one or two ideas for them to use.)
11. Once they have figured out a different way to do it next time, tell them: Great job!

This is a huge topic that I cannot cover in a few paragraphs. There are many social skills that are important to learn, including entering and leaving a group, when to talk and when to listen, how to add to the topic under discussion or change the topic, etc. There are many books on social skills that I list in "Resources."

Impact on Others

To help those with IRI, it is important to tell them how their behavior is impacting you and how most people will interpret their behavior, or they won't understand the need to change any behavior. You need to give them a string of information including:

1. When you did or said ______________________________,
   Name the specific behavior they did or thing they said and how they said it using descriptive words. Use the exact words they said and exactly how they said the words—loud, soft, mumbled, etc.—and not your interpretation of it.

2. I thought ______________________________.
   Give them your interpretation here, such as "you were upset" or "you didn't care."
3. That made me feel ____________________________.
   Use words such as mad, sad, glad, scared, puzzled, uncomfortable, etc.
4. And that leads me to want to do ____________________.
   Say the behavior you feel led you to do what you now mention, which may be to talk with them about their behavior, give them a consequence, ignore them, etc.
5. Most people would think ________________________.
   Tell them how you think most people would interpret their behavior or words, which may not be how you interpret it.
6. Most people would feel ________________________.
   Use words such as mad, sad, glad, scared, confused, bored, etc. Share what you think most people would feel, especially if you interpreted it differently and felt differently from you think most people would.
7. And others would most likely ____________________.
   Use your best guess at what actions others would take.
8. If you don't want others to ______________________ [*name the action*], you need to change your behavior, ____.
   Say the specifics of their behavior you listed above, in number 1.
9. You might consider doing this instead: ______________.
   Give them two or three ideas about behavior or words they could use instead.
10. Most people would think ________________________.
    Say how you think most people would interpret those new behaviors.

11. Most people would feel ______________________________.
    Tell how you think most people would feel about those new behaviors.
12. And others would most likely __________________________.
    Use your best guess at what others would do in response to those new behaviors.

This is how specific you need to be when people have IRI. They think differently and draw different conclusions than those who can do inductive reasoning.

Learn to ask what those with IRI were thinking and feeling in a given situation so that you know what to teach them about what happened. Give those with IRI the correct information to mend a social interaction instead of getting angry with them. Then they will be able to begin to change their behavior. They will need a lot of coaching to understand and act appropriately and not just withdraw.

For those with IRI, learn the parts of communication in sentences 1 through 4, and use them to help you be clear in what you say. Learn to say, "I'm sorry you are upset," when others get upset at you. Then ask what made them upset and see what you can learn about your behavior or their interpretations. Sometimes it's not your fault. They may be misunderstanding you, and you need to help them understand you. After apologizing, share what you were thinking that led to your choice of behavior. You need to learn to say and do things in ways that are socially appropriate (expected behaviors) if you want to have relationships that last and work well. There are many books listed in "Resources" at the end of the book that can be helpful.

Learning from Past Experiences

Most people who enter a new situation or begin working with a new person will gather information from their past experiences that are similar. They will scan what worked and what didn't work to figure out ideas about what to do now with different people and in different situations that are new. Those with IRI will struggle to learn from past experiences because their brain doesn't have a cross-reference system. Their brain doesn't pull information from files of similar experiences because similar is not noted in the files. So they will struggle to figure out possible helpful and unhelpful responses in new situations, which is basically every situation that is different for them.

You can help those with IRI by having them think back to past experiences that are similar. If they can't think of one, share one you remember. Talk about what worked and what didn't work and why. Then brainstorm two to three ideas that might work now. Share possible responses from other people for each idea to help the one with IRI choose the best behavior for the people and the situation. This helps his or her brain learn to do more cross-referencing.

Rules can also be very helpful in knowing what behavior to choose when those with IRI can't be walked through this cross-referencing process. Level 3s and below benefit greatly from rules all the time. Level 4s need to be encouraged to do this process on their own once they learn it and are in later elementary school age.

Learning from Past Experiences

Because those with IRI don't have a cross-reference system working well in their brain, they will struggle to learn from past experiences. It's important to point out their past experiences that are similar. Talk with them about what worked and didn't work and why. Then brainstorm two to three ideas that might work now helping them choose the best possible behavior for this situation and the people involved. Setting up rules to handle various situations for L3s and below can be very helpful for them to know what behavior to choose.

For those with IRI, practice thinking about a past experience that is similar to the current one when others point it out to you. Try to think about what worked then and ask if that would be helpful now. Be willing to brainstorm ideas of how to respond to others that are helpful and appropriate to the situation.

Initiating

Those with IRI are usually so busy logging information that they often don't initiate, especially in new situations, unless they are a moderate to strong extrovert or they think they are supposed to initiate. Once they know the expectations, rules, and the people involved, they are more likely to initiate contact. Their personality will begin to show, and others will connect more with them.

They may be more willing to initiate as a young child, but once they hit fourth or fifth grade, they may stop because there is so much more nuanced communication. Others expect the one with IRI to understand when he or she often doesn't understand all the communication, is working to figure it out, and then often gets left behind in conversations.

Youths with IRI may not remember to initiate but may be pretty responsive, and so others don't notice it much. They may be afraid of saying the wrong thing due to having had enough experiences of people not understanding them or misinterpreting their behavior. Not wanting to stand out or be wrong, the youths don't initiate.

Those with IRI may not know how to initiate conversation well if no one has taught them. They need to learn opening topics, how to add on in conversations, and how to close conversations. Watching and listening to another will not be enough because of their struggles with IRI and being overwhelmed with information. They need specific information on what to do and when to do it in order to be successful.

They may not be aware that they aren't initiating and how that affects relationships. They will need specific information about that.

One young girl learned rules about starting conversations and when to start conversations in fifth grade. She was an L3 and an extrovert, so she was motivated to learn to be appropriate so she could make friends. When she entered middle school, she did well because she had learned helpful rules about topics and timing. She made friends easily, even though most children with IRI struggle when they enter middle school/junior high.

There are many books listed in "Resources" that can help. Check for books that have social thinking or social skills in the titles.

Initiating

To help those with IRI, understand they often don't initiate because they are too busy logging information. Once they know the people and the situation, they will be more likely to initiate. Often they need to be taught how and when to initiate and how to carry on a conversation.

For those with IRI, you can learn to join in, carry on a conversation, and leave in appropriate ways. Find books, a good friend or family member, or a psychotherapist who can coach you on these skills. Everyone has to learn them sometime in order to function well in the world.

Asking for Help

This can be a real difficulty because those with IRI may not know when they need help. They may not realize they are struggling more than others. They may assume what they understand is correct and don't know that they misunderstood something until they miss it on the quiz or test, don't do what you want you want them to do, or don't finish all of a task that is given them. For instance, if you ask those who have IRI to put their dishes in the dishwasher, they will put their dishes and no one else's in the dishwasher. They won't put in the glasses, silverware, other bowls, etc. This can be very tiring to deal with each time. You need to tell them the definition of "dishes" is "all plates, cups, silverware, bowls, and serving dishes that everyone has used." And you may need to define it further by saying, "Pick up all the dishes on the table and in the kitchen (or all over the house as long as they can enter everyone's room) and put them in the dishwasher." It is training for each of us to learn to ask the right questions and give complete directions so they understand what is expected of them.

You won't know if they understand what they are supposed to do unless you watch them in their play or work with them on their homework. When they are young, you will have to watch and listen carefully as they play. You can add full directions while your child is playing and through example teach his or her friends to think more specifically when they ask for things or tell things to others. As your child enters elementary school, talk with your child after the friends are gone to educate him or her on the social cues and directions for play.

When the child with IRI is in elementary school, you will need to review the student's work at home when he or she is done to see if it was done according to directions. Often the child will get the first direction or two and not all the directions. It's important to coach children with IRI to read all the directions, even if they can't all be remembered. They should begin by reading the first direction and doing that one completely. Next they should go back, reread the directions, and do the second one completely. Then they should do the same with the third, etc. Or, they should read the directions and do what they can on the first page. Next they should go back, reread the directions, and do what they can on the second page. Then they should do the same with the third page, etc. When they think they are finished they should go back, read the directions again to make sure they did them all, and finish the ones they missed. The child should review directions until all the directions have been followed.

It's best to get a 504 or IEP (individual education plan) in the school that says the student can redo work if he or she does the work but misunderstands the directions. Otherwise, the grade for the class will represent what the child thought the assignment was and not what he or she actually knows. The 504 or IEP (individual education plan) can be difficult to get unless the staff is educated first about why this is needed. I have information on my website at Counsel-Heal.com and articles you can use to help educate teachers about your child with IRI. Teachers need to read this book to really understand, but frankly, most of them don't have the time unless they can get continuing education for learning it. It's important to understand that most teachers have a great desire to be helpful to students, but the resources they are given are so limited that they struggle to get all the job done during the school year, let alone learn and integrate more new things. And keeping track of twenty-five to thirty students who have very different needs is overwhelming—and even more so with a hundred or more if they are teaching middle school/junior high or high school.

You can get a lot of helpful information on the law around the country regarding education, 504s, or IEPs from Wrightslaw at www.wrightslaw.com. Some states are more helpful, and some are more combative. Most states struggle to fund education so there's just not enough staff and time to meet everyone's needs, especially as more and more children are diagnosed with issues. I try to help parents become collaborators with teachers to meet as many needs as can be met with an understanding that everything won't get done. We need to come to the understanding as a nation that education needs to be fully funded and much more creative to meet everyone's needs.

It's important for you to teach your child or children to know when they need help. They need to stop and pay attention to any question they have about tasks or assignments. It can help for them to carry around a small notebook where they can write their questions. You can set up a time for them to talk with the teacher each day about their questions. In order to see if they really understand a task/assignment they have brought home, ask them to tell you what they think they need to do. Then talk them through the steps to complete it. Ask them again what they think they need to do for the assignment before they start. This will help teach you to be more specific about directions or set up for a task. And it will teach them to be more thorough.

This is a difficult one for teens. If you teach them this process when they are young, they may use it in their teens if they are motivated to do well in school. If you check with them and they remember it and don't do it, then it's a choice they are making, and they will need to deal with the consequences. If you haven't taught them this process before the teen years, it is unlikely most teens will learn it from you, the parent. If they are motivated to do well in school, they can get this information from a psychotherapist who knows IRI or school staff that have learned about IRI.

It's important to teach language for asking for help, such as, "When you said [the words said when they were given the task], does that mean [whatever they are thinking it means]?" And if that is correct, they should say, "Thank you." If it is not correct, they need to keep asking questions, such as, "Can you give me more information?" or "Will you define that more for me?"

There are appropriate times to ask and steps to do this.

1. Tell the teacher or boss you don't understand something.
2. Ask for a time to talk with the teacher or boss about it.
3. Agree to a time to talk and show up at that time.
4. Tell the teacher or boss what you think you are supposed to do.
5. Ask the person if you are understanding the instructions correctly.
6. Listen to what the teacher or boss tells you.
7. Keep telling the person what you understand he or she is saying and asking if that is right; continue asking for further clarification until the teacher or boss tells you that you are correct.

Teens are expected to ask for help themselves, and they may not be ready or know how to ask, especially if they are L4s that didn't get diagnosed until teen years or aren't even diagnosed. Don't assume they know when or how to ask for help. If teens are open to working with the parent on this, ask them what they will be asking for from their teacher and when. Ask questions to help them get clear on what they understand and what they need from their teacher/boss. If they won't use you as a resource, have them see a psychotherapist and tell the psychotherapist you want your teen to learn how to ask for help and clarification.

Asking for Help

To help those with IRI, it's important to teach them how and when to ask for help. Help students get additional time for work or the right surroundings for tests so they can be as successful as possible. If possible, try to get an agreement in the 504 or IEP that says the student can redo work if he or she misunderstood the directions. This allows for testing what the student really knows about the subject, not about how to do the assignment. Have the student see a psychotherapist for coaching on how to ask for help and clarification.

For those with IRI, actively learn when and how to ask for help in socially appropriate ways from someone you trust. Everyone needs help at times, and so do you. Here's a process for asking for help.

1. Tell the teacher/boss/friend you don't understand something.
2. Ask for a time to talk with that person about it.
3. Agree to a time to talk and show up at that time.
4. Let the person know what you think you understand.
5. Ask the person if you are understanding it correctly.
6. Listen to what the person tells you.
7. Keep telling the teacher/boss/friend what you understand and asking if that is right and, if not correct, asking for further clarification until the person tells you that you are correct.

Thinking Differently or Divergent Thinkers

Often I find that those who have IRI think differently than the those who can do inductive reasoning. Things that would make most of us feel badly about ourselves often frustrate those with IRI but don't cause them to think poorly of themselves. They may want to do something and find they can't, but they don't attach meaning about it to themselves.

For example, one youth couldn't get his schoolwork done. He would drift off or do something fun, even though he wanted to do well at school. He couldn't make himself focus on the work, even though he had the motivation. He knew he was smart by the amount of knowledge he had. He didn't feel bad that he was failing school; he felt frustrated that he couldn't show how smart he was. Nor did he worry about what others thought about him. (That can be one of the gifts of IRI.)

Or those with IRI may feel puzzled because they don't understand what is going on but, again, attach no meaning about it to themselves. So if they need to be kept in a grade for a second year, we can't assume they will feel badly about themselves. We can't assume how they feel at all. *We have to ask them what they think and how they feel, even if they have to struggle to tell us.* This is another gift that those with IRI have for us. We really do have to let go of our assumptions and ask to learn the truth. It's as if they are from a different culture that has a different way of viewing things and a different language.

Thinking Differently

To help those with IRI, remember we all think differently. Don't assume you understand those with IRI based on your experiences, especially if you are a Feeler. Learn to ask questions to understand their point of view. *We have to ask them what they think and how they feel, even if they struggle to tell us.* And share your point of view and teach them that others think differently than they do. There does not need to be judgment about differing views. There needs to be understanding and compassion.

For those with IRI, understand that most people will not think as you do. You may be the person that solves a difficult problem that others haven't been unable to solve. Or you may see the world differently than most. Learn to communicate well and be socially appropriate, and your different way of thinking won't be a problem.

Literal

Being literal is being very concrete and specific in your thinking and language. One student got instructions in chemistry that they were supposed to determine what a compound was, based on what liquid would dissolve the compound. When she tried various liquids, she did not find one that completely, 100 percent dissolved the compound and so couldn't determine the right compound. This is one of those difficulties with a student being literal and thinking he or she understands the instructions. There was also a lack of clarity by the teacher that there might be a little compound undissolved if there was not enough of the liquid to completely dissolve it.

Some people are Thinkers who are very literal, but they can still do inductive reasoning. They will tend to make more social errors than others. But these folks will pay attention to the social situation and will understand and correct behavior in response to what they experience from another. What they say, though, will tend to be very literal. They may be able to laugh at themselves or immediately attend to another's feelings and so have far fewer problems with relationships. Sometimes they don't have much of a sense of humor and may struggle more.

Those with IRI can also be Thinkers who tend to be very literal. Those that are literal generally see things in black and white, all or nothing, right or wrong, etc. They will use very specific language and correct you when you say something that is vague. If the time is 4:47 and you say a quarter to five, they will correct you in all seriousness and say 4:47. They are not trying to be a difficult or hurtful. They are being exact in their Thinking and in their response. They will not think about how that affects the other person. They may think they are being helpful in giving the exact information because they would want that and are surprised if you are upset.

A person with IRI is often viewed as non-feeling or not caring about others because others feel hurt by what they said or did. Usually Level 3s and 4s have plenty of feelings, but they are often not based on the same reasons or interpretations as Feelers. Yes, they are usually thinking—gathering information, stating facts, and not being aware of how they are coming across to others. But Level 4s and often Level 3s can care deeply about those they are close to. They may not know how to express that well or express it in the way that particular person needs in order to feel cared about or loved. And if they mess up, they often don't know how to correct their error or repair the relationship unless you tell them or teach them. They often see what they did as right or wrong, and they may not see any other options until you give them ideas.

So, it's important to tell them exactly what behavior they did, the thoughts you had about it, how you felt, and what they specifically need to do differently in the future. You can give them two ideas, maybe three if they are older, for different behavior in the future. Any more will often make it difficult for them to remember, decide, or respond. (See the section "Their Impact on Others" on page 47.)

When those with IRI make comments, they can come across as quite direct and harsh or critical. But *they are usually commenting on the process or the information and not the person.* The comments may be about whether the process is good or bad, right or wrong, stupid or smart, etc. They usually aren't making comments about the person who came up with the process. But a Feeler will usually think it is a criticism about him or her and not the process. That person will struggle to separate the two and feel very emotionally attached to the process or what he or she has created and won't want to change much because then it stops being his or her process. This won't make any sense to those who have IRI. Those who have IRI will want to create a process that works the best for them, whether or not it makes sense to another, whether or not it will work for the other person. They may look for the most efficient and/or complete way to do things, even if it is not feasible. This can create a lot of conflict between Feelers and Thinkers.

Those who have IRI will need to pay attention to their choice of words. They have to learn ways to say things in a way that doesn't offend another person. Otherwise, the other person will become defensive or get angry, and the person with IRI won't be able to accomplish his or her goal. Learning to say "I'm sorry" is important for everyone. Those with IRI may not feel that way, but they need to learn the importance of saying that phrase to correct social errors, even if they don't understand what exactly the error was.

Feelers need to learn to say "I'm sorry" when they interpret comments to be about themselves and it's really about the process. Those with IRI often feel as if a Feeler dumps his or her feelings on them. It can be very surprising, and they have no idea what to do with the person and their feelings and their interpretation which is so very different than their thinking. Feelers need to apologize for dumping their feelings on the Thinker. They need to learn to hold their feelings and check their interpretations before reacting. They, not the Thinker, are responsible for the feelings that led from their interpretations.

Our society has mostly been filled with Feelers, and therefore, responding from our Feelings has been the accepted norm. But as we gain more Thinkers in our society and fewer Feelers, we need to understand that both have to apologize for their assumptions or the way things are said.

Literal

Those who are literal or logical often come across as not having feelings because of how they state things. They generally make comments about the process that are heard as harsh and critical by Feelers.

To help those with IRI, understand they need specific information in order to learn to say things in a way that is not damaging to relationships. Help them to understand that most people respond from a feeling place and to interpret things to be about themselves. If they apologize for their wording, it can help reconnect them to the person. Then they can explain that they weren't making a judgment; they were talking about the process. This can help Feelers to shift to the issue away from their making a judgment about themselves, which the Thinker was not thinking.

They need to learn there is more than one way to do things or understand things, and they can allow another to have his or her way, even if it doesn't make sense to them. They also need to learn to identify their feelings and share them in ways that are not damaging to relationships. Feelers also need to learn to apologize for their assumptions and reactions. They are often wrong about what the IRI Thinkers are saying or meaning. Feelers need to learn to hold their feelings and check their interpretations before reacting.

For those with IRI, everyone has his or her own way of doing things that makes sense to that person's brain. Understand that each person thinks a little differently. You won't know what the other thinks or feels unless you ask the person. It's important to learn how to say things in ways that help others to hear your input. Learning to say "I'm sorry" to people who get upset at you can help diffuse their anger. Learning to share how you are thinking can help others to understand you.

Perfectionist

Some people demand that things be done to their level of perfection. It usually appears in their repeated attempt to do something just right. They may find it difficult to finish and turn in homework they don't feel is perfect. Or they walk away from a task because they can't master it to their demanding level.

Some people with IRI have this issue. You can talk with Level 4s about what most people will accept as good enough and explore what good enough would be for them and set some rules. They may need help to know what to say to themselves in order to let go of needing it to be perfect and to know how to feel content. Level 3s will need you to help them know what is enough or not enough, and you will need to oversee their work process. They will need help to think about and accept what is good enough. They also need help to know what to say to themselves in order to let go of needing it to be perfect and know how to feel content. Level 2s may have a very difficult time understanding there is another way to do things or that they could have a different rule. I recommend professional help who will also tutor the parents in how to work with the child. Or get a psychotherapist or IRI coach if you are an adult.

Those with IRI generally won't have much or any ability to be empathic. They will be rigid and won't see anything outside their world view when dealing with others. This can be very difficult to deal with as parents, a partner, or a boss. You will have to be clear with the person who has IRI about what you or the job needs and the expectations. Those with IRI can be upset by the consequences and will have to learn whether their need for perfection or the consequence is more important. If the consequence is one they don't want, they will need to change their behavior and expectations. They will need coaching on how to do that.

I find using kinesiology, energy psychology, or energy medicine modalities in therapy to be the most helpful for this issue.

Perfectionist

The reality is that nothing is perfect. We are all human. We all have different ideas of what is perfect. And we all make mistakes.

To help those with IRI, they need to hear this information and they need help from a psychotherapist to shift their behavior when they get stuck in having to have things be their idea of perfect.

For those with IRI, understand you will rarely get the time and energy to do something to your idea of perfection. Others won't understand why you need to do it. You do need to learn to move on from a task and settle for good enough instead. Get help with this issue from a psychotherapist that understands IRI.

Resistance to Change—Possible OCD

Most of us get tired of the same old thing and look for change by buying something new or trying a new activity or going on a vacation, etc. For those with IRI, each situation is new. They have to work harder, and it takes longer to figure out each person and each situation. It's far easier for them to have the same friends, to go through the same routine, to eat the same things, to wear the same clothes, etc. They constantly have to deal with what is new for them. They can take in only so much information or change—which is true for all of us. *So they look for things to stay the same the way most of us look for something new.*

Often those with IRI need to know what the schedule is ahead of time so they can prepare for transitions and for the demands of various situations and people. Some, generally the extroverts, can transition more easily than others. It's important to pay attention so you know how much you need to tell them ahead of time and how soon you need to tell them. Some need to know the night before, and others the morning of so they can remember more easily. They aren't trying to be difficult; they are trying to manage what can be overwhelming for them.

One older child asked his parents where they were going and when they were going to be home whenever they left the house. This was his way of managing the change. At first, he was very troubled and anxious if a parent was late. The parents were able to give him more of a time spread (for example, "somewhere between four and five"), which helped, but he still became somewhat anxious after five o'clock. The parents then began to text when they couldn't meet the exact time frame and gave him a new time frame. Even if they had to do this more than once, it seemed to work to keep him from becoming anxious.

Sometimes another part of the brain is not working as well, and it does lead to obsessive compulsive disorder (OCD). People with IRI often need a routine to manage all the information input in their life. But those with OCD aspects demand the same routine every day without any changes ever and get very upset if it is at all different. They have thoughts they can't stop thinking. And/or they compulsively have to do the same thing in a situation until they meet satisfaction. They need a psychotherapist who knows how to work with OCD to help them. (See the section "Differential Diagnosis" in the chapter "Diagnosing.")

Those with IRI who do not have OCD aspects will do the same thing because they may not know another way to do it. If they are offered another option and the reasons for it, they can often adjust, some more easily than others. They may feel anxious about learning the new option, but once they have learned it, they won't continue to be anxious. It's important to work with them to expand their repertoire of options, even if it leads to anxiety initially. Teaching them to identify their anxiety and then coping methods for it can be very helpful. There are behavioral ones and energetic ones. (See the section "Stress, Worry, Fear, Anxiety, and Panic" on page 98.)

Having a mega-rule that they have to make some changes each year can help. Then creating a new rule or sub-rule in various categories can allow them to make smaller changes. (See the section "Mega-rules, Rules, and Sub-rules" on page 88.) Having coping skills for anxiety will help them manage the change well. When the accommodation does not demand too much of others around those with IRI, it's important to accommodate them but not completely, or they will not survive in the world. You need to push their level of comfort to expand their abilities. Working with a therapist who understands OCD can help with techniques, but you may have to educate the professional on IRI.

Again, you have to ask the right questions to make sure why the one with IRI is choosing the same behavior, routine, etc. Psychotherapists need to really explore what a person is *Thinking* and *Feeling* when he or she is choosing a behavior. We can't assume anything.

Resistance to Change—Possible OCD

Change happens all the time. It's important to accept that.

To help those with IRI, it's important they learn to manage their anxiety about change. Teach them ways to identify stress, worry, fear, etc. and how to cope with and relieve those feelings. It is also helpful to keep most things stable so they know what to expect and can be more relaxed. Telling them or reviewing a calendar of events at the beginning of the day helps them know what is coming throughout the day and lowers their anxiety so they can function better. If a large change is coming, share it several weeks ahead and make plans for when and how to do all the things that are needed for that change.

For those with IRI, there is nothing wrong with wanting the same things. You will have to deal with change, so learn how to manage it and the anxiety that comes when change happens. If you have obsessive compulsive behavior, get help from a professional.

Imagination

Some people think that those on the autism spectrum have no imagination. This may be true for some who are very literal. Those who struggle with inductive reasoning and aren't literal will still struggle to be able to understand what others are imagining in their play or their story. They will have their own great story going on in their mind. But because it doesn't match what others are imagining, they will struggle to join in the play of others.

Those with IRI will assume that others think the same way they do because they can't imagine anything else. So if those with IRI join the play or the story of other children, they often appear to take over the play because they function only in their own story or what comes from their own imagination. They struggle to think the way their playmates think. It's often not a control issue (although it can be if the situation is new and they are stressed/anxious) as much as an inability to think the way others think. But others experience it as controlling and will often back away or get into a fight in some way. If other children understand that the child with IRI isn't trying to control but is struggling to join in, they may have compassion for him or her. Instead of shutting the child out, they may invite the child to join in in some way. They will need to know how to give the child enough information that he or she can join in the play. The person with IRI will need coaching on social skills to join a group and to leave a group. Again, the section "Mega-rules, Rules, and Sub-rules" can help. See also "Resources" at the end for books on social skills.

It's important to explain to a child with IRI that often others think differently than he or she does. Encourage the child to watch the play and see what the rules are that others are using. Or suggest the child follow and copy what others are doing in order to join in. Let the one with IRI know he or she can suggest another idea once or twice in play but must go with what the group is doing in order to be a part of the group. Most of us automatically do this, and we don't even think about it. But for those with IRI, they need to be taught these kinds of rules in order to be able to join in and function well with others.

It's also important to both affirm their ideas, thoughts, feelings, and creativity while also sharing your thoughts and feelings that are different from theirs. Help them to understand that other people have their own thoughts and ideas.

Children use so much technology today. When they play games online or through consoles connected to TVs, it is mostly side-by-side play. That makes things easier for those with IRI. They are not managing as much information input so they are less overwhelmed. They may spend a lot of time on technology as a way to be with their peers and not be overwhelmed, especially in the teen years. For children and teens with IRI, it is appropriate to let them have more time gaming than you would a child who can do inductive reasoning. Have them earn gaming time by doing their chores, completing school work, and being a part of the family. Don't let it control their life. Give them some gaming time in down time (see "Down Time" section) and some as a reward.

Imagination

To help those with IRI, know they often lack imagination on a level with others. They find it difficult to be able to imagine what others are doing, thinking, or feeling and the reasons why. That can make it difficult to join in others' play or conversation. Having someone explain what others may be thinking or imagining can help immensely. Coaching them on how to join in play or conversations can be very helpful.

For those with IRI, understand that others think and feel differently than you do. They have different needs and wants than you. Learn to ask what others are doing, feeling, thinking and then think about what you would want if you felt or thought that way. It can help you know how to join in a group or conversation. Check out the book on conversation starters in the resource section. Some are appropriate and others are not.

Memory

We have three types of memory: short-term memory, working memory, and long-term memory. Short-term memory is information that is coming in at the moment.

We choose what goes into working memory based on what we need to do now or in the very near future. Working memory allows us to add information while holding onto and manipulating other information. If you are logging a lot of information, you may miss transferring instructions or learning from short-term memory to working memory. You will then struggle to get the tasks done because you don't have all the instructions in working memory.

What is transferred to working memory may happen sporadically, based on interest, energy, or the number of instructions. It can be confusing to parents and teachers when students have incredible memories and focus but can't manage more than two or three instructions at a time. These students will often struggle to keep themselves organized. It seems incongruous or that the child doesn't care. Either is an incorrect interpretation.

A person with IRI is working hard to gather information from the warehouse of the mind to figure out how to do the first task and so often can hold only one or, perhaps, two tasks in mind. The individual may have the beginning pieces of a task in working memory but lose the later pieces. He or she will need some kind of reminder of all parts of a task in order to fully complete the task. This requires getting written instructions that can be continually reviewed until each part of the assignment is checked off. If the individual doesn't get written instructions, he or she can ask for them or can take notes on the instructions. The person with IRI needs to learn to try to write exactly what people say. Try to have the person develop a shorthand for notes that allows for writing things down more quickly. The first sentence a teacher says usually explains the task. Later sentences will explain how to do the task. Get permission to check notes with the teacher, parent, or boss to make sure the one with IRI is understanding the assignment.

Often those with IRI struggle with transferring information from short-term or working memory to long-term memory. Long-term memory is what we can recall several hours or days from now. One student seemed to learn math very easily and got good grades on his homework. When he took the tests, he only made Cs. When asked, the student indicated he wasn't anxious about the test. When he was evaluated, he got additional memory testing done. What became apparent is that he could easily take in the information in short-term memory, work with it in working memory, but didn't transfer it to long-term memory. That student had to keep reviewing math consistently to retain it as he learned more each year.

Repetition can help as with everyone. Those with IRI may understand how to do something the first time they learn it but then not transfer it from short-term or working memory to long-term memory. Thus, they have to learn it all over again, which they do easily. The frustration comes with not being able to retain it. It can be confusing to a parents or teacher when they understand it so quickly but can't retain it. Everyone may feel confused or irritated. *It is a memory-transfer issue, not a learning-the-information issue.*

For some people, memory is better held visually. Those people will remember faces but not names. For others, it will be auditory, and they will remember names better than faces. Some focus on physical sensations like tastes or touch and will remember things associated with that. Some people with IRI will have only their thoughts. They won't use their other senses fully because to do so is overwhelming. One of the things that can happen when those with IRI get older is they begin to dump memories or learning because they are managing so much information. I've seen this some with teenagers when they go through puberty or those with bipolar as well. We all do this naturally over time, but it may happen much quicker for those with IRI since they consciously have to figure out so many things. I wonder if their working memory area of the brain is much larger than the brains of those who can do inductive reasoning.

Some supplements can help with memory issues. See a naturopath or nutritionist for more information.

The Positives about Poor Memory

Sometimes there is just too much to remember through the years, so teens and older folks with inductive reasoning issues will begin to dump those files and boxes. One young woman said to me that it's not so important to hold onto old memories, especially the painful ones. She said she is making new memories that are much more pleasant to hold onto and remember. She decided to get rid of old journals and some pictures that only brought up negative memories that she hadn't remembered for several years until she was reminded. So sometimes having a difficult time remembering can be a blessing!

If you want to keep more of your memories, it's good to save pictures and look through them periodically to reinforce the positive memories. You can keep important memories by writing a short review of your week at the end of each week. Then review it monthly to help hold important memories.

Memory

We have three types of memory—short-term, working, and long-term memory. Short-term memory is what we are taking in at the moment and we sort by importance—deciding what will go into working memory, go into long-term memory, or be ignored. Working memory allows us to hold some information while we manipulate other information. Long-term memory is what we can recall several hours or days from now.

To help those with IRI, understand they have difficulty managing their working memory. They may be able to handle only two to three directions or pieces of information and manipulate them at a time. They need written instructions and training to review them for completing each part of the task. They may not transfer information from working memory to long-term memory and may need to relearn the same thing over and over. They will learn it quickly but not retain it, so constant review will be needed. It can be confusing to teachers and parents and frustrating to the student. *It is a memory-transfer issue, not a learning-the-information issue.* Teach them to develop ways to keep track of tasks, timing, and instructions. We all do those things and need to do them in order to be functional.

For those with IRI, be sure to write down instructions exactly as they are said. Figure out a system for keeping information on what to do that you can refer to easily and quickly, like notes on your phone by date and task or a calendar with reminders. Work on accepting if you have a memory transfer issue and compensate for it by regularly reviewing what you are learning. The positive side is that it may be easier for you to forget painful or difficult memories and move on in a positive way in your life.

Attention

Mel Levine studied the learning process and identified parts of attention as:

- attending to,
- planning,
- organizing, and
- monitoring what you say or do.

If you have IRI, you are often attending, and you are attending to detail until you are overwhelmed, and then you shut down. This doesn't even allow for moving to planning. If you come to a quieter moment, you may be reviewing information in order to understand it. If you can't make connections between pieces of information, it is difficult to plan and to organize information. With a lack of being able to prioritize information, it is difficult to organize it. If you can't read your own body or learn to hear yourself inside your mind, instead of out loud, it will be difficult to monitor what you say.

Planning and organizing can be difficult when you struggle to make connections between pieces of information. Developing specific strategies for planning and organizing can be helpful. Teachers usually give you directions at the top of the page or at the beginning of a verbal assignment. You will need to remember to review the top of the page for the instructions on written assignments each time you come to the end of the task in order to see if you did everything that was required. And keep reviewing until all the task is complete. For verbal assignments, you should take notes. Again, review your notes each time you think you have finished a task to make sure you did everything that is required. See if you can audiotape instructions from teachers or bosses so you can review it later for all the information.

Make a to-do list and keep a calendar to remind you of things you need to get done in the future. You will also have to remember to look at them. It can help to develop a routine for looking at your list or calendar, like after each time you eat. Or set a watch or cell phone to beep at certain times of the day that fit your schedule and allow you to review the tasks. Set your alarm to remind you far enough ahead of time so that you can get to places or get the task done on time. It will help you to develop routines, like putting your wallet or purse or keys in the same place whenever you come home. These types of routines help everyone to keep track of things.

Learning to write down questions when they come to mind so they can be asked at the appropriate time can be very helpful. That way, you won't forget them because you have moved on to other information. Carry a small notebook and pen/pencil, write down verbal directions, and check them with the person giving them for accuracy. This one can be difficult because you may miss more information while you are writing. You may be able to quietly use a handheld recorder or your cell phone for notes or questions. Sometimes teachers or bosses can be asked the question right away, and that makes for more consistent hearing of directions. Other times, they can't, and the question will have to be held until a later time.

In order to do any task, you need to be able to do the following things, which Mel Levine listed on his website, www.AllKindsOfMinds.org:

1. Predict an outcome to guide your actions or strategies (previewing).
2. Inhibit a first response in order to think about the best strategy to guide production (inhibition and facilitation).
3. Utilize an understanding of time and effort to enhance efficiency (tempo control).
4. On-going quality control of work (self-monitoring).
5. Activate past experiences to guide current actions or strategies (reinforcement control).

If you have IRI, you will struggle with all these items. There are ways to cope.

Previewing may be difficult since you often don't connect similar things when you have IRI. You may have an excellent memory but not connect things you learned in the past to what may work in the present. You can ask a parent or partner to help you remember similar situations you have dealt with in the past. It will be important to review what's happened after an interaction or the completion of a task. Note what you have learned and develop a rule or sub-rule that will help you to remember to do it even better in the future. Ask your parent, a good friend, or a partner to help you review things and learn what you need to do differently. No one can figure everything out on his or her own.

If you have IRI, you may be pretty good at holding a response while you think of a strategy. But it may take you longer to think of a strategy, or you may need to ask for help on a strategy in order to know what is socially appropriate. Practice figuring out two to three ideas on your own on how to solve a problem and then check out the ideas with a safe person like your parent or a partner. If you can't think of any ideas, then ask for help. Don't wait until the problem becomes more of a problem. Take action as soon as you get home or can talk with a safe person in your life.

If you are helping those with IRI, tempo control can be an issue if it takes them longer to do tasks than others in school or at their job. They may be struggling to find the right information in their memory, so they are slower at processing, and it can seem they are inattentive. Or they may be missing hearing information because they are sorting through their memory instead. Because information doesn't always get moved from short-term or working memory to long-term memory, they usually can manage to remember only two to three directions. These children need more processing time, and they need help with organizing and follow-through on tasks. (See the "Organization" section on page 80.)

Students can get an IEP or 504 at school for extended time to complete tasks. Parents will likely need to remind teachers of that, especially in the upper grades so that your child can get it. You will have to review your child's work, which they may not want you to do. If that is the case, then just send out a reminder or call in a reminder quarterly to the teacher(s) about what's in the IEP or 504. You can also request an IEP or 504 meeting at any time. It will take them a little time to coordinate with the staff, but they are required to meet with you if you have requested it. The website www.wrightslaw.com has many resources about the law and education that can be helpful, including their book, *All about IEPs*.

For those with IRI, you will almost always have to abide by the time constraints at work. You may have to choose work that allows you to be more flexible in getting tasks done in certain time frames. You may need to get help to figure out how to do tasks in ways that work for you. You may need help to figure out how to talk with a boss or teachers in order to get permission to do things your way. Or you may need to learn why they have you do tasks in a certain way so that your brain will follow their instructions. It can help to have someone talk through these issues with you to help you understand and make a plan of action. Working with a psychotherapist or parent can be helpful.

Self-monitoring can be difficult. You may need to set time to review your work or behavior to determine if you need to change anything. You may need to find a friend at school who will help you do this. As an adult, you may need a partner or a psychotherapist to help you do this. You often won't understand how your behavior affects others, so you will need help for this, especially at first. If others respond to you in unexpected ways (see Garcia-Winner), then you should check out what happened and what other people meant by what they did or said to you. Write something that will help you remember and then bring it to someone you feel safe with that can help you sort out what is going on. Or find a psychotherapist you can trust to work on this issue.

Reinforcement control can be very difficult if your brain doesn't do inductive reasoning well. You will not be making the connections between the past and similar situations in the present. Having a parent, friend, family member, or partner point out a similar time and what worked for you that time can be helpful. Setting up a rule to know what to do can also be very helpful.

Learning appropriate social behaviors is crucial to functioning in society. Understanding expected behavior versus unexpected behavior that Michelle Garcia Winner talks about in *Social Behavior Mapping* can be very helpful. Learning mega-rules, rules, and sub-rules and using them to help organize your thinking and responses can be very helpful.

Attention

You need to be able to do the following in order to complete a task:

- attend to,
- plan,
- organize, and
- monitor what you say or do.

Those with IRI may do the first very well but struggle with the following three. There are strategies for remembering, taking notes, and monitoring that can help. Review the above information or check out the website www.AllKindsOfMinds.org for more ideas.

Organization

It is difficult to organize things if you struggle to attach meaning or priority to things. Meaning is something you attach to things for a variety of reasons—like/not like, interesting/boring, need to know/no need to know, etc. You can help children set priorities in their work, self-care, family interactions, play, etc. that will greatly impact them as they grow older. We all do this for children, but with those who have IRI, you will need to be much more specific. Using mega-rules, rules, and sub-rules can help them begin to organize their thinking and information retrieval. (See the following section, "Mega-rules, Rules, and Sub-rules.") It can give them guidelines for how to do many tasks, as well as social interactions.

For example, they will usually cram everything from school into their folder or backpack and not care that things get crumpled or misplaced. You can help them set up a file system, but they generally won't know how to file unless you teach them. Have a set of rules to help them file.

1. Mega-rule: put your name and date on each paper and file it each day in your binder.
2. Rules
    a. File work that needs to be done in one file in your binder.
    b. File work completed in a second file. If the child is older, the rule is to put each subject paper into each subject file.
    c. Turn in the work in the completed file at the beginning of school the next day. (Elementary students will have reminders for this generally.) Turn in the work for each class in at the beginning of the class for older students.
3. Sub-rule: Organize the papers in the files by the date the paper is due.

If the teacher can remind students to do this at the end of the subject time, it will really help them. If you set this up early in life with good explanations of how it can help them, then they may work to do it throughout their school years (Level 2 and 3 and maybe 4.) Junior high and high school students will be expected to do this and will not receive reminders.

Often smart L4 kids won't need this system until they hit middle school/junior high. If they haven't been taught before then, they are often not in a place to learn it until after they finish puberty. They may be highly motivated to do well in school and ask for help, at which time you can teach them. Otherwise, you will need to wait until their brain has settled down hormonally—generally around tenth or eleventh grade. If they have been taught and have used it in the past and are not using it now, then assume they are choosing not to do it. (See the section "Teens and Their Development" on page 114.)

Organization

It is difficult to organize things if you struggle to attach meaning or priority to things. Meaning is something you attach to things for a variety of reasons—like/not like, interesting/boring, need to know/no need to know, etc. Using mega-rules, rules, and sub-rules for organizing tasks can be a very helpful way to organize information.

For those with IRI, learn to use mega-rules, rules, and sub-rules to help you organize information for easier retrieval. It can help you organize and complete tasks thoroughly without missing anything important. School or work will be much easier and without as much anxiety if you can learn to use this.

Time Awareness

For those with IRI, time awareness can be affected. When they are tracking so many individual pieces of information, they may not track or may not be able to track time as well. When it is difficult to attach meaning to something, it is difficult to remember it. When it is difficult to attach a priority to something, it is difficult to remember it. So they may not be able to tell you how long something happened, i.e., how long they heard the alarm going off, how long they felt something, how long it took them to do their homework, etc. They may not be able to tell you if it happened a week ago or a month ago. They are not lying or trying to make less of a negative thing they have done. They often are just not tracking time or connecting it to other pieces of information about the day or the people involved so they can recall accurately.

If you have IRI, it can help to do a week in review each week. Use a weekly calendar and note the dates for each day, the events in each day, and notable things in each event. These are the three layers, date, events, and notable things in the event. If you put things in three layers, it can help you remember and learn to layer information for easier retrieval. You can log this information daily very quickly, or if you struggle with time at the end of the day, you can do it weekly.

If you are a parent of a young child with IRI, begin with noting days, dates, and events. As the child grows older, you can add things to this type of journaling, like the amount of time spent at the event or task, how the child felt at each event, what he or she liked or didn't like, how the child handled certain things like a conflict or stress, etc. This can be a way to note what works for and what doesn't work for the child in managing feelings, relationships, or time.

To help those with IRI become more time aware, use an analog time clock where you can see time passing. Get a timer that you can set for timed tasks, such as homework, chores, etc., that shows a red dial slowly disappearing as time moves forward. They may need to guess how much time a task takes, log the actual time, and review that with you. This will allow them to find out if they don't track time well and if they need help. Then you can plan together the type of help they can use, like plan out the time for the day ahead of time for tasks and for fun. Agree to reminders or set additional timers for breaks, etc.

Some people with IRI find a weekly or monthly planner overwhelming. They can't shut out the need to do all the tasks, and they feel a tremendous amount of stress until all the tasks are done. Those people should use a daily planner that shows only one day at a time. They can log what needs to be done or the timing to do it in future days, but they don't have to see them all at once. If they struggle to manage time, you can help them plan for time in the week by organizing each day ahead of time, but they only have to see one day at a time.

Students may need to have a 504 or IEP that gives them extra time for tests or handing in assignments if they are lacking time awareness or it takes them longer to process and do their work. They will need more oversight from parents in the younger years to set up good time habits. Teachers need to work more with parents who need to do this kind of oversight with older students. Learning to manage time is critical to being successful in the world.

Time Awareness
To help those with IRI, remember time awareness is difficult when they are managing so many pieces of information that they see as having little or no connection to one another. It can help them remember things if you review the day at the end of the day and the week at the end of the week. A 504 or IEP that allows for more time on assignments can be helpful. Letting them learn to sense time by using a clock and a timer where they can see time passing can help.

For those with IRI, guess how much time a task takes, log the actual time, and review the difference. Be willing to use strategies that will help you manage time well. You will have to do it in order to function in the world. People expect you to be on time to your job and complete tasks when required, or you will be fired and have no money to live—unless you can figure out a way to make a living without having time awareness.

Over Focus

Those with IRI can have extreme focus. It may be a way to manage getting a task done and not being distracted by all the input they experience throughout the day. It may be their brain's way of relaxing to some degree—only thinking about one thing at a time. Sometimes (for L2s and some L3s), their brain just has one interest to the exclusion of all else. In 2016, we don't know yet exactly what area of the brain controls that or why.

You can have those with IRI take breaks in their work for play and in their play for work. This encourages them to increase their ability to shift focus and to be OK with not finishing all of one task. This happens all the time in school. This can be a huge challenge for some but a necessary life skill. It also can teach them that both play and work are important and that there needs to be a balance between the two. They may have anxiety to deal with when they shift. Teaching them a coping tool for that can really help.

Over focus can show up by having only a single interest that they spend all their free time thinking about (L2s). In school when they have a single interest, they can learn to read using books about their single interest. You can have them write about their single interest. They can find out the history of their single interest. You can encourage them to follow a similar thing to their single interest or perhaps a tangent off their single interest. For instance, if trains are their single interest, you may be able to get them also to study the rail system and where it goes and which trains use what rails in order to learn geography. Anything that expands their learning and their options will increase their ability to manage the world as an adult.

Shifting focus can create anxiety for some. See "Stress, Worry, Fear, Anxiety, and Panic" on page 98 to find out ways to identify and manage anxiety.

Over Focus

To help those with IRI, understand they can have extreme focus as a way not to be distracted or because their brain is wired that way. Help them to broaden their focus by exploring tangents off their single interest. Have them practice shifting focus and managing any anxiety that arises from that.

For those with IRI, understand that most people cannot focus the way you do and don't expect them to do it. Also understand that it's important to have more than one focus in order to survive in the world. Try to figure out how to make a living using your focus of interest, or learn a new interest.

Lack of Focus

A lack of focus can cause difficulties in school for children. To complete a task, it takes focus. You need many moments in a row to start, work on, and complete a task. And you are required to do many tasks in a day.

Often those with IRI are diagnosed with ADHD inattentive when they lack attention. The *Diagnostic and Statistical Manual of Mental Disorders* really explains ADHD. My belief about those with ADHD is that the fight-or-flight response is on all the time and they can't turn it off. The constant scanning makes it difficult to pay attention beyond the moment. Those with ADHD are impulsive but can do empathy upon reflection. See my website, www.Counsel-Heal.com, for more information on ADHD.

That is not the case for those with IRI. Those with IRI function in the moment because they are very busy logging everything they can and, when overwhelmed with information, can't always pay attention to everything or follow through on tasks. They often struggle to hold more than two or three directions or information in their working memory in order to complete a task. It's important to review the directions for tasks and teach them that once they are finished they are to go back and check to see if they did everything the directions said. Having a quieter place for test-taking can help. Once they know the task, they can often do it if they are motivated. Explaining the purpose for doing each step can help them. Explaining how they can use the information they are learning can be helpful. Figuring out rewards, like teaching them to feel good about completing a task using praise from themselves or from an adult, can motivate them. Getting a reward like tokens that they can save up and use to get something in the future can be very helpful for younger children.

Some young adults with IRI will have a lack of focus and take longer to figure out what they want to do with their life. If they follow rules when they are young, they will do what is required of them. As they grow older, they may need more help. They may not have any ambition and may need to have family or a counselor help them think through what they like and don't like to do, what they want to learn more about, what they think and feel about school after high school, and how they want to survive once they graduate.

Sometimes parents have to be very direct in telling the older child with IRI he or she has to figure out a way to survive without them but also work with them to make a plan and follow through on it. They may have to set limits that the youth cannot live with them after a certain age, after college, etc. in order to motivate the individual to prepare for life outside the family. You should start this process in middle school or junior high. This can be a complex issue to determine the youth's abilities, needs, and course of action. It can help to work with a psychotherapist on this so an appropriate plan can be made that will help the young adult be successful. This can be difficult and scary for the parents. Grief will be a part of the process (see the "Grief" section in "Resources"), and parents will need support, too.

Some supplements can help with motivation, and seeing a naturopath or nutritionist for information on what to take and dosages can be helpful. There are some medications you can get from your doctor or a psychiatrist. You will have to deal with side effects with almost every medication and sometimes with supplements. Educational or developmental kinesiology or energy medicine can help, and you can find out more in "Resources."

Lack of Focus

To help those with IRI, understand they may struggle with focus because they are logging a lot of information. Without the ability to prioritize, they will struggle with knowing when not to log information and, instead, focus on the task they have.

Often those with IRI struggle with transferring information from short-term memory to long-term memory. They often struggle to hold more than two or three directions or pieces of information in their working memory in order to complete a task. It's important to review the directions for tasks and teach them that once they are finished they are to go back and check to see if they did everything the directions said. Having a quieter place for test-taking can help. Having rewards for finishing tasks can motivate them to stay more focused.

Sometimes young adults with IRI do not have much focus and need help to plan for life after high school and living on their own. Start this in middle school or junior high. The family will need to determine the level of help that's needed for the one with IRI to become an independent adult. Working with a psychotherapist to determine the appropriate expectations and the individual's abilities can be helpful. Parents will need information about grief and support through their grief.

For those with IRI, find a psychotherapist that can help you plan for your future. It's important you have work you can do that allows you to become an independent adult where you can pay all your own bills. You cannot assume your parents or other adults will take care of you for the rest of your life.

Mega-rules, Rules and Sub-rules

Those with IRI often take in information as single pieces of data that aren't connected by meaning, priority, or similarity. So they usually make rules to understand what behavior they should use, who they should believe, when they should do tasks, etc. It can help them to have levels of rules since their brains don't prioritize well. You can organize information into categories using mega-rules, rules, and sub-rules in order to access information quicker and more accurately. Those below a Level 3 may have to have additional instructions laid out for each sub-rule, depending on their abilities. Teach them to review the mega-rules first to find the category, then the rules to find the situation or people involved, and sub-rules for the specifics.

It can help to both tell and make a list of leveled basic rules for elementary children. You may have to use words and pictures for younger children. For example:

Mega-rule: Clean yourself every day

Rules:

1. Wash your hands and face when you get up, if the child is young.
2. Shower or bathe every day, if the child is older and with sub-rules of:
    a. Wash your hair.
    b. Wash your face.
    c. Wash your neck.
    d. Wash your chest.
    e. Wash your arms.
    f. Wash your underarms.
    g. Wash your back.
    h. Wash your belly.
    i. Wash your private parts.
    j. Wash your bottom.
    k. Wash your legs front and back.
    l. Wash your feet top and bottom.
3. Brush your hair.
4. Clean your ears.
5. Wash your hands after you use the toilet.
6. Brush your teeth after you eat a meal.

You may have to sub-group the sub-rules if the child can't manage more than two or three directions. For example, the sub-group "head" could contain "hair, face, and neck"; "body" could contain "chest, back and belly"; "arms" could contain "arms and under arms"; etc.

Level 2s and 3s may need even more specifics about what tasks it takes to wash their hair, i.e., "Get the shampoo, get your hair wet and then move out of the spray, squeeze your palm full of shampoo, put it all over the top of your head, rub it into your hair from the center of the top of your head out to your ears and from the front of your head to the back until all the hair on your head is covered with bubbles, put your head under the spray until all the bubbles are gone, and now you are done with washing your hair.

If they don't develop a complete routine about something, they will miss parts. They may carry that incomplete routine with them the rest of their life without awareness. And those missed items may make a difference as to whether they fit in with their peers or stand out in odd ways.

For tweens and teens that have developed more in their awareness of self and others (L4) and have the routine above already memorized, you may have a list that says the following.

Mega-rule: Clean yourself every day

Rules:

1. Shower or bathe every day and clean every body part.
2. Shave.
3. Brush your hair.
4. Put on deodorant.
5. Put on lotion or makeup.
6. Wash your hands after you use the toilet.
7. Brush your teeth after every meal.

You may not need the sub-rules if the tweens or teens already have routines in place or are advanced enough in their awareness that they don't miss parts. You will have to observe and offer guidance to the amount they will listen and accept it. This may seem ridiculous for those of us who did not have this issue growing up. But doing this can be a real gift to your child who struggles with IRI and will help them fit in with their peers. Teens will often not want to hear any of this from parents starting sometime in junior high until sometime in high school. They are separating and learning to function without you, and reminders from you can often make them irritated. Their peers may have to point out when they stink because they haven't used deodorant or have worn their socks too long, etc.

Mega-rules, Rules, and Sub-rules

To help those with IRI, give them mega-rules, rules, and sub-rules to help them learn to organize data by groups. It can help them organize the warehouse of their mind so they can find information easier. It can help them know how to complete a task thoroughly.

For those with IRI, learn to use mega-rules, rules, and sub-rules to help you organize information for easier retrieval. It can also help you organize and complete tasks thoroughly without missing anything important. Ask others to help you set these up if you don't know all the steps to complete various things.

Behavior Issues

All children have behavior issues to varying degrees depending on what behavior they have learned at home, what developmental task they are working through, and how their brain is functioning generally or that day. Lack of sleep or even allergies can cause anyone to be irritable.

Often when expectations are too high, children will act out. When children are overwhelmed, for whatever reason, they will act out.

Feelers will calm down if you learn to acknowledge and address their feelings before problem solving.

Behavior issues happen for a variety of reasons for those with IRI, including:

- Typical reasons all children act out
- Not being able to identify their feelings
- Not being able to identify feelings quickly or easily enough to manage them
- Not being able to identify the level of their feelings
- Not knowing how to express their feelings appropriately
- Not being able to tell how their body is behaving when they have various feelings
- Not being able to hide what most of us hide in order to get along with one another
- Difficulty knowing how to respond in social situations
- High stress due to having to figure out everything consciously
- Not having coping strategies or ways to reduce the stress they feel

As a parent, you can learn how to deal with your child's feelings and behaviors from many books not specific to IRI. I highly recommend anything from Jean Illsley Clarke, Elizabeth Crary, Michael Riera, and Daniel Siegel. Parenting those with IRI can be a very different issue because defining feelings and body sensations and knowing what to do with them can be very difficult for those with IRI. Jed Baker's books are excellent, and he really understands IRI. Michelle Garcia Winner's books are also excellent.

Defining Feelings

There are reasons that we have feelings. They give us information about what is happening with our self or in relationships with others.

Our feelings guide us on what we need to do in relationships. Many of us were raised that some feelings are good and some feelings are bad or we shouldn't have them. Or some feelings were ignored, and others were focused on. This limits our information and appropriate response to situations. It's important to have *all* our feelings and learn to experience and deal with them well.

We get mad when someone invades our boundaries. If you are a young child, when you own a toy, it is yours, you can do what you want with it (within reason), and that is the boundary. When someone takes your toy without asking you and acts as if it is his or her toy, that person has crossed your boundary. And you want to defend your right of owning your toy so you feel angry. You have choices about what behavior you use at that point. You can yell at the other child, "That's my toy," you can grab it back, you can scream or cry, you can tell an adult, etc.

You may set a goal for yourself and not meet it and feel angry at yourself. You can say mean things to yourself, but that won't help you meet the goal or feel good about yourself or make you want to meet that goal again. You also have to learn to treat yourself well. You may need to look at the goal and have help to see if it is a realistic goal. You may need to change the goal. You can figure out what you did that wasn't helpful in meeting the goal and change that particular thing so you can meet the goal. You can say encouraging things to yourself so that you try to meet the goal again. There are many ways to manage anger that are important to learn. There are many books listed in "Resources" to help you learn.

Sadness comes when we have lost something. Perhaps you are really enjoying doing something, and you have to stop to eat, do a chore, go to bed, etc. You will need to be able to identify sadness and tell others who are in your family that you are sad. Then they know, and they can help you with your sadness. Some grown-ups know how to deal with sadness, and some don't. Some people are Thinkers and will problem solve but won't know how to be emotionally supportive. If you are a Thinker, you will do that too. You will want to problem solve and may or may not be aware of your sadness. If you are a Feeler, you will need help to deal with your sadness. You will need to have someone hear that you are sad and tell you they understand why you are sad and perhaps hug or hold you. Those are the common ways to manage sad. You may need different ways to express it. Some people play music that sounds sad to help them feel their sadness. Some watch a sad movie to feel their sadness and possibly express it. Some people draw a picture of what they lost or their feeling of sadness. It's important to find a way to express your sadness that works for you. And it's important to share it with a partner or parents so they understand you and your behavior when you feel sad.

Gladness is generally always accepted. Most people feel happy when someone smiles at them. When you feel glad, you usually want to smile. Occasionally, someone grows up in a family where it isn't accepted. Then you need professional help from a counselor to learn to be aware of your gladness and how to express it well. And that can be true with all feelings you struggle with.

Scared is what you feel when you are threatened—when something comes at you that scares you or someone makes a statement or gesture with an intention to inflict pain, injury, or damage either physically or emotionally. It may be a response to something you did or something the other person thought you did but you didn't actually do it. You may get tense and want to fight or flee (run away). That is our body's normal response to feeling threatened. It's important to know how to handle someone else's anger or a situation that makes you feel scared. How quickly you want to respond depends on the level of scared that you feel.

Because those with IRI often struggle to make meaning, they may have more difficulty defining their feelings. Beginning to label those starting at age one can really help. Giving them words for levels of feelings as they get older, then words for opposite feelings, and finally words for a combination of feelings can be helpful in understanding feelings and their relationship to each other and the situation. Feelings can be about a person or a situation or the environment.

Those with IRI often freeze, which is also the initial fight or flight response. You stop and look and listen intently using all your senses to determine if there is actually a threat to something that startled you. Those with IRI may be doing it in response to something they are startled by or because they are trying intently to understand what is happening in the situation.

I sort feelings into mad, sad, glad, and scared for elementary school ages. I also give titles to the levels of feelings so the children can learn to express themselves more appropriately. A level 0 = neutral/no feelings/quiet inside for every feeling, and level 4 is the most intense feeling.

✻ Levels of Feeling Mad

1. **Irritated or annoyed**

   You want to frown, and you don't like the behavior of someone, but you can ignore it unless it gets worse.

2. **Frustrated**

   The behavior or situation has continued, and the person won't quit, and you aren't sure how to make the person stop or make the situation different. Your shoulders and arms feel tense, and you want to shake the other person or stomp.

3. **Mad or angry**

   You want to push away the other person, scream, or move away from the person. You feel invaded, and you want it to stop— NOW.

4. **Rage**

   You are so mad that you don't think you can control your own behavior, and your hands move to fists. You may act to hurt the other person who is doing the behavior you don't like before you think, and you will have to deal with the consequences.

Levels of Sad

1. **Down**

   You feel a little low on energy and not happy or maybe have no feelings.

2. **Sad**

   You feel as if you want to cry, your chest is tense, and you may or may not cry. If you do, it will usually release the tension in your chest, and you will feel better.

3. **Depressed**

   You feel sad most of the time, and you have a hard time wanting to do anything .

4. **Despondent**

   You feel so sad and hurt so much inside that you don't want to live any more. Thoughts of dying are common.

Levels of Glad

1. **Positive**

   Things look physically bright, and you feel as if you want to do things.

2. **Glad or happy**

   You feel as if you want to smile and you may do it, and your chest feels open or relaxed, and your stomach feels warm.

3. **Joyful**

   You feel so glad that you want to move your body—like skip or dance and smile or laugh or sing for a little while.

4. **Ecstatic**

   You feel so warm and joyful that you can't be still. Energy rushes throughout your body, and you have to do something like jump or dance really energetically.

Levels of Scared

1. **Uncomfortable**

   Something makes you want to pay attention more. You may look around to try to find out what makes your body feels as if it wants to twitch.

2. **Scared or fearful**

   A shot of energy runs through your body, and your eyes open wide. You don't want to be around the person or in the place that is making you feel afraid. You feel as if you want to fight the person or flee (run away) from the place or person.

3. **Anxious**

   You have ongoing fear with tense shoulders and stomach. You want to avoid whatever has made you scared, and you feel tense until you can avoid it. You can't relax for long periods of time.

4. **Terror or panic**

   You feel so scared that you can hardly move your body. You tend to draw in your limbs and bend over your belly. You will do anything to avoid what is making you scared.

It is good to describe overwhelmed since if you have IRI you often feel that way. Overwhelmed is what you feel when you have too much information or feelings coming too fast. You don't know what to do with the feelings or how to manage the information or how to respond. You can feel weighed down or want to hide, freeze, run away, get angry, or cry in response. Getting time to yourself can really help. Avoiding some situations or planning for when and how to leave other situations can help.

There are many books for kids to identify feelings. There are some online games, board games, and apps for identifying feelings as well. Google "identifying feelings," and you will get many pictures and games.

Defining Feelings

I've organized feelings into four groups—mad, sad, glad, and scared—with four levels for each feeling. It's important to learn to identify feelings because they give us information about how relationships are working. Feelings tell us important information about what we need to do differently or what others need to do differently in our relationships and when change needs to happen. It also tells us what we are doing well and what we might want to do more in our life or relationships. It is helpful to know the levels of feelings so that we know how quickly we need to respond and what choices we can make.

For those with IRI, at first, you may find it difficult to identify feelings—both your own and those of others. You will get better at it as you practice. Our feelings give us important information about what we need to do in relationships with our self and with others. Get help to understand and work with your feelings.

Stress, Worry, Fear, Anxiety, and Panic

I find that many of those with IRI don't really know what I mean when I ask them if they are anxious or stressed. And they are often anxious many times a day or whenever they are in a social situation. So, I put together the following information to help them identify when they are having stress, worry, fear, anxiety, or panic.

* Stress

Stress can be positive or negative for our body. Small amounts of stress can be beneficial and desirable. Positive stress can motivate us to get something done in a specific time frame that benefits us. It can improve things like athletic performance or acting. You feel it until you begin to do the task and then use that energy to help you complete it. It can help us adapt and react to the environment to keep us safe or in good health. Too much stress makes us physically sick and over time wears our body out so that we have a disease.

Stress can be felt as:

1. Tension or pressure often in the neck, shoulders, or stomach
2. Nervousness
3. Feelings of insecurity
4. Loss of appetite or wanting to eat when you aren't hungry
5. Headache or migraine
6. Overall irritability, everything bothering you

You may experience the following with too much stress for too long because you move in and out of worry and anxiety many times a day:

1. Ongoing anxiety
2. Feeling overwhelmed
3. Exhaustion
4. Social withdrawal
5. High or low blood pressure
6. Skin problems
7. Insomnia (not being able to get or stay asleep)
8. Lack of sexual desire (sexual dysfunction)
9. Gastrointestinal problems (constipation or diarrhea)
10. And for women, menstrual problems

And too much stress over time may cause more serious conditions like ulcers, irritable bowel syndrome, heart problems, etc.

Worry

Worry is thinking negative thoughts about a time in the future or trying to get ready to handle an event or person that has affected us negatively in the past. When we stop thinking about it, we stop feeling worried.

Fear

Fear is a Feeling response to a perceived threat that you are Thinking about. Sometimes you are aware of the thought, and sometimes you aren't until you stop and realize you are afraid. You want to try to escape and/or avoid the thing, person, or situation that scares you, or you want to fight. Fear comes with the thoughts, but once you process the thoughts, you can let go of the fear. Your body moves into the fight-or-flight response, which includes:

1. Eyes dilate (to take in more information).
2. Heart rate increases.
3. Blood pressure increases.
4. Blood flow to the major muscle groups increases (in order to run or fight).
5. Immune and digestive functions decrease to provide blood to the muscles (which, over time, keeps us from breaking down and utilizing food).
6. Perspiration increases.

If you can't stop thinking about the fearful situation or person, then you are moving into anxiety.

Anxiety

Anxiety is thinking negatively about a time in the future or trying to get ready to handle an event or person that we don't know anything about, that we may not know how to handle, or that has affected us negatively in the past. Anxiety is ongoing without much of a break. Someone who has anxiety might also experience it as a sense of dread or panic.

Signs of anxiety include:

1. Heart palpitations (a heartbeat that ranges from often unnoticed skipped beats or accelerated heart rate to very noticeable changes accompanied by dizziness or difficulty breathing)
2. Tachycardia (fast heart rate)
3. Muscle weakness and/or tension
4. Fatigue (overall tiredness)
5. Nausea (feeling sick to your stomach, as if you're going to throw up)
6. Chest pain
7. Shortness of breath (the feeling that you can't catch your breath)
8. Stomach ache (from tension and lack of blood flow)
9. Headache (from tension and lack of blood flow)
10. Difficulty concentrating
11. Tunnel vision (generally due to blood flow leaving the head to more critical parts of the body in defense)
12. Hyperventilation (fast, heavy breathing)

External signs of anxiety that others may see include pallor (lack of color in the face), sweating, trembling, and pupillary dilation (eyes dilate open to take in more information). Those with IRI may not be aware of them.

Panic

Panic can take the form of panic attacks, which are periods of intense fear or apprehension that come on suddenly and are relatively brief in duration. Panic attacks usually begin abruptly, reach a peak within ten minutes, and subside over the next several hours.

Symptoms include:

1. Trembling
2. Heart palpitations
3. Chest pain (or chest tightness)
4. Shortness of breath
5. Light-headedness (a feeling that one may be about to faint)
6. Hyperventilation (breathing faster or deeper than normal)
7. Dizziness or slight vertigo (a whirling or spinning sensation of movement)
8. Hot flashes (a feeling of intense heat with sweating and rapid heartbeat and typically lasts from two to thirty minutes)
9. Cold flashes
10. Sweating
11. Nausea (feeling sick to your stomach, as if you're going to throw up)
12. Numbness (not feeling parts of your body or skin)
13. Burning sensations (particularly in the facial or neck area; the face flushes like when a person is embarrassed)
14. Paresthesia (tingling, burning, pricking, or numbness of the skin)

15. Sensations of choking or smothering (obstruction of the flow of air from the environment into the lungs)
16. Difficulty moving
17. De-realization (the perception or experience of the external world seeming unreal or you seeming unreal)

Sometimes those with IRI don't have all the information they need to understand why they should not worry or be fearful. We have to understand what is making them worried by asking enough of the right, detailed questions. Then offer them ideas about how to think about the situation differently or plan for it differently. They may or may not be able to believe it. Once they are finished feeling afraid or anxious, review with them what happened and discuss whether what they feared actually happened. If it didn't, then how should they feel next time? If it did, then what can they, and possibly you, do differently next time to make things easier or better? Always work out loud with them and write things down so they can read and review it.

We all try to avoid that which scares us or makes us anxious. Many times we can't do that so we have to learn to cope with our fear or clear it. Those with IRI can't avoid the information overload and the anxiety that comes with social situations. **It's vital for them to learn ways to relax.** And the ways that work for them may not be the ways that those who can do inductive reasoning would use. It's important for them to experiment to see what really allows them to relax. Encourage them to try a variety of things and place what they try in three categories:

1. Works really well to relax, and I couldn't do it in public
2. Works to any degree to help me relax, and I can do it in public
3. Doesn't help me relax

If you struggle with being in touch with your body, you will need help to become more aware of the body sensations you are experiencing. You can tense each body part and then release it to feel what it is like to have tension and then not to have tension. Or a parent, relative, or friend can squeeze each body part (not private parts in the genital or breast area) and then release it to help you be more in touch with your body. An outside observer (parent, sibling, teacher, or friend) can tell you what he or she is seeing and encourage you to do calming strategies. The sooner you notice tension from feeling anxious or afraid, the sooner you can do something to calm your system. This may allow you to handle social situations better. None of us handles social situations well when we are really tense.

For those with IRI, the stress level is much higher in any social situation. They really need help to manage stress and anxiety. You or they can plan for some things to lower their stress. They often need to leave sooner or have recovery time after any social event. Planning for this and/or for breaks within social situations can really help. Having a role in social events can make things less stressful.

Make plans to manage the stimulus. At home, children and teens can go to their room. They need to know how to leave and how to enter the family or other social situations (see "Mega-rules, Rules, and Sub-rules" on page 88). Have them practice this at home. You can coach them to do it well so they are successful when they use it out in the world.

Parents need to plan for breaks for children when they are out in the world. Young children can have the rule that they can hide under a blanket in the car when they need to have quiet for a while. Finding a quiet corner and having a book or game to focus on can be helpful. Find restaurants that have less stimulation. Going to the movies may be a quieter way to go out for teens. Anyone can go to the bathroom for a while and sit on the stool in order to be alone and quiet for a time, even if he or she doesn't use it. Learning some coping tools for the body from kinesiology or energy medicine can be very helpful. Use tools from the *Relaxation and Stress Reduction Workbook*. Have several options for in public and at home depending on the age and circumstances.

I've seen young children hide under tables at a restaurant to avoid input. I've seen a child leave his birthday party, go to his room, and close the door to recover. This family did not know their child had IRI and wondered what the problem was and what to do. There are lots of options to manage the amount of information input. The more you can recognize it, talk about it, and develop ways to manage it, the better the person with IRI will function in the world. There are many books for children about feelings in the "Resource" section.

Stress, Worry, Fear, Anxiety, and Panic

There are levels of stress, worry, fear, anxiety, and panic. When you have a lot of fear or anxiety it is vitally important for your physical and mental health to learn to identify it and to release it and relax your body every day. Learning some coping tools for the body from kinesiology or energy medicine can be very helpful. Using tools from the *Relaxation and Stress Reduction Workbook* can also be helpful.

For those with IRI, learn to check in with your body. Know what physical sensations indicate what feelings. Learn to identify what level you are feeling and the appropriate action for you to take in the social situation. Or learn to leave the situation appropriately and then deal with your feelings. Practice ways to calm your body and mind regularly.

Frustration

Most people with IRI get frustrated a lot. They are working hard to learn how to be in the world, and the demands are very high to understand others and to fit in with others. They may get frustrated with:

- Being interrupted in a task before they are finished
- Being asked to remember too many instructions at one time
- Finding the right information internally to respond to others
- Finding the right words to explain what they are thinking or feeling
- Themselves when they can't do something easily that they think they should be able to do
- Doing things that they don't see any reason to do (including homework when they already understand the concepts, even if they can't do the work, i.e. Math)
- Another when the person doesn't understand or is slow to understand what they are saying when it's perfectly clear to the person with IRI
- Another's lack of understanding that they are working very hard all the time and need to not be pushed or have too many demands
- Not understanding others thoughts, feelings and motivations

They often lash out when they are frustrated and then don't see the impact that it has on others. And yet we don't understand how our requests or demands impact them. We are treating them like people who can do inductive reasoning, and their brain cannot or cannot do it well. It's so important that we all understand what is going on in how those with IRI process information. We all deal with people in our lives that have IRI, and we often don't know. We just demand they act and be just as we are when their brain is wired differently. It is neither their choice nor their fault. And we often misinterpret them. We attach meaning to their behavior that is not accurate, and we respond from that assumption, and we are wrong. And those with IRI struggle to understand those who can do inductive reasoning. It's as if others are talking a different language with different rules from the one those with IRI use. One older man resigned himself to just accept things that he didn't understand and set them aside so that he stopped being so frustrated.

Frustration

To help those with IRI, understand frustration is often their response because they are very stressed in social situations. We need to learn not to react to it and help them identify and handle it well. Teach them to tell others when they are frustrated and to apologize when others feel hurt by their frustrated reaction.

For those with IRI, learn to identify when you feel frustrated. Get help to learn to manage it well. Be ready to apologize when you say something harshly because you are frustrated. Learn to share when you are frustrated before the tension builds too much and you say or do things you don't want to do or that lead to consequences you do not want. Others may be able to help you with whatever is frustrating you, so learn to ask for help.

Depression

Almost everyone has experienced depression at some point in life. It's a part of the human condition. It is important to get help from your doctor, psychiatrist, or naturopath and a psychotherapist to help with the depression. The vast majority of people cannot get themselves out of depression by themselves. *If you feel that you really want to hurt yourself or want to die, you need to get professional help immediately and likely take some standard medications. Don't keep suffering. Call 911 or your doctor.*

Symptoms of depression include the following, which are experienced most or all of the day:

- Feelings of emptiness or hopelessness (younger children may be irritable)
- Lack of interest or pleasure in all or almost all activities
- Fatigue or quick loss of energy
- Struggle to concentrate or focus
- Struggle to get to sleep or sleeps too much
- Struggle to make decisions
- Feelings of worthlessness or extreme guilt
- Weight loss or weight gain with or without much change in eating levels or patterns
- Thoughts of death with or without plans of killing oneself

Depression can be caused by:

- The things you are thinking
- The way your body is functioning
- Ongoing stress or trauma

A psychotherapist can help you look at how you are thinking about things and help you to change your negative thinking patterns about you or about others. Energy psychology, educational kinesiology, and EMDR (eye movement desensitization and reprocessing) are faster ways of changing negative thinking.

It's important to find out and deal with how your body is functioning. Our body's hormonal balance is affected by:

- Negative thinking
- Exposure to trauma
- Lack of proper nutrition
- Lack of vitamin D
- Exposure to toxins
- Other hormonal imbalances, like puberty, menopause or pregnancy
- Sleep issues, including sleep apnea
- Digestive issues or allergies
- Stress, especially ongoing stress

Trauma happens whenever we experience something that is shocking and involves a loss. It can be emotional, physical, or sexual in nature. It could be your pet died. Or perhaps you slipped on ice and fell hard. Or maybe someone touched you sexually when you weren't expecting it. It's important to get help from a psychotherapist or pastor to resolve the trauma.

Lack of proper nutrition happens when your digestion isn't working well. Working with a naturopath whose specialty is nutrition or a nutritionist can be helpful with digestion issues. Your body won't get what it needs to function well until your digestion functions well. The book, *Brain Maker* explains all about this. Most medications for depression affect the digestion in negative ways.

Taking vitamin D, getting out in the sun, and/or using full-spectrum lights can help raise your vitamin D levels. Taking vitamin D with omega3 has been found to act like an anti-depressant for some people. St. John's Wort has helped many with depression. See your doctor or naturopath to have your vitamin D level checked to see if you need supplementation. You can take standard medications for depression, which often have side effects that you will have to manage. I talk more about health issues later in the book.

Toxicity exposure deposits things in our brain or body that affect our hormones. There are ways to clear toxins from your system. Or you can be allergic to things and not be aware of what you are allergic to. Working with a naturopath or a Defeat Autism Now! (DAN!) physician can be very helpful. There are a couple of books worth reading—*Children with Starving Brains* by Jacquelyn McCandless and Jack Zimmerman and *Non-Toxic, Natural and Earthwise* by Debra Lynn Dadd.

Most of us have issues with sleep at times in our life. Lack of sleep is one of the main reasons for ill health. You may have trouble falling asleep, staying asleep, or waking early due to a variety of things. You may sleep too much. When we have a lot of stress, it can affect our cortisol levels, which regulate waking and sleeping.

It's important to get blood work done to see what may be happening. There are a variety of tests that can be done. An ND (naturopath) can be most helpful in determining what is happening in your body. An MD (medical doctor) will only be looking for disease, and your body may not be there, yet. Be sure to tell them anything that you are taking, either medications or supplements (pills, tinctures, or teas), because there can be interactions between them, side affects you are experiencing, or you can be taking too much or too little of something that is helpful and it can have a negative impact.

It's important to get a sleep study done if your blood work is normal and you still struggle with a lot of fatigue. Sometimes people don't breathe well through the night and wake up to various degrees. You may not be aware of waking. It is called sleep apnea. You may not breathe well at night because of your body structure or because you are overweight. Your back, neck, or jaw may be out of alignment and cause restriction, and a chiropractor or other body worker may help.

We all think negatively at times. You can think negatively about:

- Yourself
- Your abilities
- Other people
- Others' abilities
- Particular situations
- Particular places

It's important not to get into the pattern of thinking negatively. Negative thinking causes tension and unhappiness. Over time that can cause you to become ill, either temporarily with a cold or with a disease if the tension and negative thinking are ongoing.

It's important to learn to recognize when you are thinking negatively and work to change the pattern. Working with a psychotherapist, doing DBT (dialectic behavior therapy) in a group, or working with social skills can help. There are many forms of therapy that are beneficial for changing negative thinking. See the resource section for more information.

Depression

To help those with IRI, remember all of us get depressed at times. To set a good example to family members with IRI, get physical and emotional support to change your depression or help you with your grief. Tell older children and teens that you are getting help and the reason you are getting help. You shouldn't go into details with children, as they won't know what to do with the information and it could be overwhelming. But knowing that going to see someone that can help you is good information for those with IRI. Work with a psychotherapist to change your negative thinking patterns about yourself or those with IRI. Parents need to notice and plan for lower stimulation or retreat options for their children. And teach them socially appropriate ways to do them. Learn and use techniques to manage stress and anxiety so you can teach those who have IRI to do them or do it with them as a family.

For those with IRI, it's really important to pay attention to your thinking and correct any negative thinking patterns. Get help from a psychotherapist to learn to do that and to clear trauma. Get help from your naturopath or nutritionist for any digestion issues, to clear toxins, and to check your vitamin D levels. Those who live in the Pacific Northwest, other areas with long periods of overcast skies, or latitudes that cause significant dark times of the year often have vitamin D deficiency. Take some if you need it. Talk with your doctor about any sleep issues you or others notice about you, like snoring at night. And most of all, learn good ways of coping with stress through body or breathing exercises, changing your thinking patterns, supplements or medications, good eating, good sleep, or energy exercises to cope in the moment.

Confusion

Those with IRI feel this a lot of the time because they can't read others' body language or do empathy. It is so common they probably don't think about the fact that they are confused. They see it as a regular way of being. They might not be able to identify it unless someone has helped them label that feeling. It can cause them to be slow to respond or give up if they are too confused or confused for very long.

Helping them to identify the feeling of confusion and exploring what causes them to feel confused can help both of you understand what the difficulty is about and decide how to find out what they need and resolve the issue.

One older man said he put some things that would take too long to figure out, or that he decided were just not a priority to figure out, in the boxes that he labeled "I'll never understand that." He would then ignore them unless the issue kept coming up. Then he might change the priority for dealing with it. He was very good at organizing and prioritizing but struggled to understand others' thoughts, feelings, and motivations. Once he got help from someone who understood IRI, he was able to begin to take more things out of those "I'll never understand" boxes and get help to understand and work with them along with the person they were related to.

> **Confusion**
>
> *To help those with IRI,* remember that they are confused a lot and may not be able to name that feeling. Helping them to identify the feeling of confusion and exploring what causes them to feel confused can help both of you understand what the difficulty is about and decide how to find out what they need and resolve the issue.
>
> *For those with IRI,* find someone who can help you identify when you are confused and can explore what is causing your confusion. Those who have read this book or understand IRI can help you determine what you need and how you can get your need met so that you are not longer confused.

Teens and Their Development

Biologically most teens enter puberty in middle school. Hormones are constantly changing over a year or two as their bodies adjust to becoming an adult. I find that those who have IRI are often affected much more than those who don't. Their brains struggle more with the hormonal changes because they are already struggling more than the average person due to stress. Stress has a huge effect on our hormonal balance in our brain and body. That is why it is so important to help them know about stress and anxiety, be able to identify those reactions in themselves, and explore what helps them before they hit puberty. Trying to figure out coping mechanisms at puberty is next to impossible because they are shifting around so much they can't tell what works and what doesn't. Parents can really worry about how their child will ever manage in life. Is this how they will always be? I want to reassure you that this is a couple-year process and they won't stay in that scrambled place. *Everyone gets better.*

It's at this same time that communication becomes much more nuanced, and those with IRI will struggle more because of it. Peers also become the main focus for teens with IRI, and they won't want to listen to a parent. It can be a dramatic shift for those with IRI. Yet they will also struggle more with their peers in missing social cues. This may be the time that IRI shows up if they are a Level 4. It can be a very difficult time. Do get support as a parent and see if your teen will accept support from other professionals since he or she won't want to hear anything from you. Teen years are much more intense and difficult for those with IRI.

Teens are beginning the separation from parents. They are working to figure out who they are separate from their family so they can go out into the world with confidence. Seventh and eighth graders are often very oppositional as a way to separate. This can cause difficulty when they don't understand social cues. Parents need to let their teen fail so he or she learns. This can be difficult especially when social cues are missed. You can offer to share your insights if your teen wants them on a regular basis and is allowed to take them or not. Learn to share insights in non-judgmental ways that are calm so your teenager can hear them better.

Those who have IRI and begin puberty may feel like an adult, even though they aren't ready to take care of themselves at an adult level. This can cause major conflicts with parents. A parent can gently ask if they are able to support themselves (listing all the tasks and knowledge that they don't have yet) when the teens act as if they can make their own decisions without any input from parents. Remind them that you are there to help them get ready to leave and that means that in some things (like safety issues) they will have to listen to you and abide by your rules until they leave home. Teens will often recognize at some point (fifteen years old or later usually) that they can't do it on their own and will become very appreciative of what you do for them. This may come later for those with IRI. A great book for understanding the teen years is *Uncommon Sense for Parents with Teenagers* by Michael Riera. It walks you through what is normal and helps give you an idea of what is going on when teens are so uncommunicative.

Sometimes parents will need to be very direct and harsh before a teen with IRI will hear and accept limitations or consequences. It can be very hard on parents to have to be so direct, be so specific, and lay out realities and consequences. It's best to work with a psychotherapist who understands IRI who can coach you on when and how to do this.

One teenager, when he entered puberty, acted as if he was an adult and could make all his own decisions without regard for anyone else. That parent had to yell that he was still a child, could not support himself financially yet, and did not know all he needed to survive in the world. The parent was the adult, and the teen needed to follow the rules at home that were set for his safety. He needed to still learn many things before he was ready to be out on his own. After hearing all that, the teen backed down with a great deal of resentment, but did follow the family rules. Once he got a little older, he let go of the resentment because he came to see his parent was right. It was very difficult for the parent to yell all that, especially when she never imagined she would parent that way or need to parent that way.

Teens may become very hypersensitive in their responses. Working to say things gently and specifically can be very helpful. Again coaching from a psychotherapist can be very helpful.

Teens with IRI will be one to four years behind their peers in social abilities, depending on their Level of Impact. It's important for a parent to be realistic about expectations for teens. They will need more down time to relax and to process. All teens need this, but these teens need it more. All teens withdraw to their room and spend time figuring out who they are. Don't add extra chores when they hit puberty. Let them know you are giving them a break for a few months and then reassess. We want them to learn to take care of themselves but not until they come out and want to connect again. First they have to know who they are before they will be motivated to take on more tasks of self-care. Then gradually add some chores. Remember they are working probably four times harder in social situations than you are. And don't let this break go on too long, either. They need to learn to manage their life. Don't let them withdraw and game for hours on end for months or even years.

Teens and Their Development

To help those with IRI, understand all teens are learning who they are and how they want to be in the world. It is difficult to go through puberty, and we need to give them time to manage it and to think. Those with IRI will be much more stressed and scramble more hormonally that others. They will often come across much harsher in their communication than their peers. But everyone gets better. Please remember that and don't get discouraged. Do remind them of appropriate social behavior when they will listen.

> *For those with IRI,* it can be hard in puberty when you and others are changing all the time. It can be extra stressful, and you need ways to manage your stress that work well for you. Do keep learning about yourself and what you like and how you want to be in the world. Recognize that your parents need some information from you to keep up with the tasks they are to do as parents and providers. Answer their questions with at least a neutral attitude if you can. You have some time to get ready to be an adult in the world. Try to let adults know if they are demanding too much from you, and negotiate for what you need. Get help from a psychotherapist who understands IRI who can coach you and them.

Ways of Coping

Besides changing our thinking or behavior, we all need ways to cope with our feelings and find ways to relax our body. It is important to learn a variety of ways because different times and situations allow for different options.

Gaming

Many parents are concerned about teens or young adults who stay in their room and play computer games all day. Most teens disappear to varying degrees for a couple of years as they figure out who they are separate from their parents and family. Those with IRI generally need more down time and some time where they are successful at something that doesn't require figuring out the rules. Most games are pretty clear about rules and goals, and those with IRI are successful at them. This can be a huge relaxation mode for them after working so hard to figure out things all day around people. I think this time is vitally important to them. If you struggled all day and then came home to do something you were really good at, wouldn't you want to spend time making yourself feel better about yourself and more relaxed? Anyone would. I think it is important they have some chores and time with family that brings them out of their room periodically. But we need to give them more time gaming than we do the those who can do inductive reasoning.

I suggest up to an hour of game time after they get home just to relax and feel better. Then having gaming as an incentive to finish a task (homework or chores) can be helpful. Alternate work time and play time so their body can relax periodically. Setting a timer for both work time and play time can be helpful. Those with focus issues may find it easier to finish a task and then game and then finish the next task. Help them divide work into various tasks or steps so they know when to take a break. Elementary children should work for up to thirty minutes and then break for fifteen; teens should work for forty-five to sixty minutes and then break for twenty to thirty minutes. All should get up and move their body during the breaks so their muscles will release the tensions that have built up—and "all" does mean all of us. I suggest one to two hours total online gaming on the weekend for those who can do inductive reasoning and up to four hours if homework and chores are completed for those with IRI. It's best for their body if it's not one big chunk of time, but broken into several between various homework and chores.

As a parent, you will have to decide the level of violence that you allow your child to see and participate in the games. But understand that those with IRI aren't necessarily affected like children who can do inductive reasoning. They aren't going to feel the empathy that impacts most of us negatively when we see violence. At the same time, if they think it is normal to have violence, then they should not participate in violent video games.

I remember when my son was young and our family played video games. If I flew off the road in the game, I was stressed. I was really stressed by bridges falling away from under me into nothingness. I watched my other family members, and they were not stressed as I was. I am highly empathic. So how people react to violence in games is different for everyone. Some people will get stressed, and some won't.

It's not necessarily tied to inductive reasoning. You really have to ask each individual if he or she is stressed by the game, discover what in the game stresses the person, and talk about how he or she will handle it and how much time is good for the person to experience that stress. I personally don't agree with allowing viewing of realistic-looking blood and guts. That's where I drew the line when my son was young.

There are studies that have been done that indicate there can be an addiction to gaming because of the positive hormones it stimulates. This is especially true when there is no break in the play. Those with IRI need to be taught social skills and various options for down time and relaxation. If they don't get that training, they will likely choose to keep gaming because they don't know anything else that makes them feel good. They may also need help to identify stress in their body, stressors in their environment, and ways to manage them. (See the "Stress, Worry, Fear, Anxiety and Panic" section on page 98.) It's really important to determine the level of IRI, their ability to monitor their stress, and teach them a variety of ways for release and relaxation.

Gaming

To help those with IRI, understand that gaming can be an immense stress reducer for them. It can be a way of increasing positive hormones in their system. Use it as a reward for their finishing school work and chores. But also give them down time where they can do it for an hour or so after school or major social situations they attend. Make sure they learn other ways to relax, release the stress, and feel good about themselves.

For those with IRI, gaming is a great way to relax. It's important that you don't set up an addiction to it that keeps you from developing good social skills. You need to practice social skills around people to be good at them like anything else you learn. So even though it is stressful, plan for some people time on the weekend, even if it's just your family.

Taking on a Role

Because those with IRI often struggle with social skills, they tend to take on a role or task so they know what to do. If you give them a task in a social situation, they can be doing it while social interaction goes on. For example, at a larger family gathering, they could serve the food or take the plates away and put them in the dishwasher. This allows them to be part of the group without having to say a lot or keep up a conversation, especially if they are an Introvert. These children can be given things to hand out at school. They still need coaching, but why not let them do something that will ease their anxiety during times that should be fun or relaxing? Every moment doesn't have to be a moment of learning.

Help them to develop roles they can switch from and to depending on the situation. Help them define the tasks and what people talk about who have that role.

All teens try on different roles and ways of behaving to find out what fits for them. Teens who have IRI and those older may find a role they want or like to play. It could be the brain if they are smart, the rebel if they don't do work they think isn't worth doing and their peers admire that, or the class clown if they are funny (yes, some actually can be). In the work world, they may choose to be a salesperson or a teacher or a scientist, and they will focus their energy on doing the tasks of that role very well. They will tend to talk only about information related to that role, and you may have to help them shift roles, focus, or topics at home.

> **Taking on a Role**
>
> *To help those with IRI,* understand that they can be helped by having roles and knowing what to do in various settings. You can give them a role when they are young or have them watch and decide on a role for themselves when they are older. You can talk together about what that role does and how that role acts.

For those with IRI, choose a role and try doing it. See if you like it and what you get from others for doing it. Decide if you want to keep it or not. You may want to try on different roles to see how they feel and fit. And try them in different situations to see what works the best in that particular situation. It can be a fun thing to do.

Down Time

Those with IRI can get sick more often than most because they are working so hard socially that they are more stressed than others. What's true for everyone is that the more stress you have, the more likely you will get sick. It's vitally important that those with IRI have enough down time where they are alone and don't have to work at social interactions. This is crucial to their well-being. It can be hard on the rest of the family members who want to relate to them or do family things. But *those with IRI are working two to four times harder all the time* when they are around people. If they are introverts by nature, they will rarely want to spend time in groups of any kind outside of immediate family because of the amount of information they have to manage coming from each person they see and how it drains them. This is not a social fear. Groups are an overwhelming experience because there is so much information moving so quickly among so many people that the person with IRI can't track it well. If they are extroverts, they will handle time among people better because they gain energy from being around others that compensates for the intense work they are doing. One man learned not to try to understand some social situations and just let information pass him by so that he was not overwhelmed and stressed.

Those with IRI need down time to themselves to recover, so plan for it. They also need down time to process all the information they have collected that day. And they need down time to figure out themselves. After they get home from school or work, *don't ask twenty questions* about their day. Ask them how they *felt* about their day and then allow them TV time, Internet time, video game time, reading, music, or whatever works for them to relax and not Think. What they choose to do to relax may not be what we would choose, but respect their choice. Parents, do try to get children to try a variety of things to reduce their stress as some work better at school or work and some work better at home. After down time, you can ask a little more about their day. Sometimes planning to ask only three to four questions can keep you from overwhelming them. You can do this two or three times in a day.

Down Time Ideas

Down Time and Younger Children

Preschool and elementary school children need some down time when they get home. Thirty to sixty minutes is common. Social interactions are simpler, less nuanced when you are younger, and your system is more resilient. I've seen the amount of down time increase in the teen years and then decrease as people get older. Help younger children do a variety of things in their down time so they have options they know as they get older.

Down Time and Teens

Teen years are very stressful with the addition of hormones and figuring out intimate relationships. If you add the additional piece of IRI and managing more nuanced interaction to it all, you have social processing that is four to eight times harder for teens with IRI. So give them a break and enough recovery time. *Teens will disappear into their rooms for long periods of time.* You may want to check in for a few moments after each hour or two to find out how they are doing and if they are doing their homework, etc. Be sure to let them know ahead of time that you are going to do that. But it's important to learn to leave them alone. This may be an unexpected loss for a parent that he or she needs to grieve (see the "Phases of Grief Explained" section on page 202).

Teens may appear depressed to the parent when they are just processing or recovering. If you are concerned about depression, then ask them. You may have to give them a definition and behaviors that fit for depression. Those with IRI that can't monitor their own body cues well won't be able to lie well. Those that struggle to monitor and know what their body is feeling will struggle to know if they are depressed. You will see how they are really doing in their body/facial cues, even if they don't tell you the truth. And those that are literal won't lie. If they tell you they are feeling depressed, then you can help them or get them the help they need. Sometimes medication works well. Finding a therapist that understands IRI is very important since traditional talk therapy about feelings doesn't work well with those who have IRI. They usually find it very irritating and unhelpful. They need practical tools to identify feelings and ways to track them that are scaled in a simple way, i.e., none, some, moderate, a lot, so they (and you) know what's really happening. They also need training that is very behavioral and practical on how to deal with their feelings. They need training on social thinking and how to do it.

Down Time for a Parent Who Has IRI

Down time is particularly hard for parents with IRI. Their partner and/or child or children will want to see them when they get home and spend time with them. It may work best for parents with IRI who work outside the home to take some time in the car or stop somewhere before they get home to do things that lower their stress and doesn't require social interaction. The amount of time and where they stop for down time should be negotiated with and communicated to their partner ahead of time. Parents with IRI need to learn to give at least ten to fifteen minutes of connection time with their partner and/or child or children. Young children need a little time with their parent right when they first see them. Longer time, perhaps around dinner, can be spent with the parent with IRI. The partner and/or child or children need to learn to give their parent with IRI down time. Parents with IRI need to learn to come back out and reconnect to their partner and/or child or children again after they have recovered some. Partners may have to *plan connection time* to manage the issues of family, work, house, or their relationships.

Parents who manage the home and have IRI will need down time to recover during the day. When the children are young and at home all day, childcare, dance or swim lessons, etc. can be time they can take to themselves in the car or at home. Or trade off childcare with a friend. Make sure stay-at-home parents with IRI take down time and don't do household tasks or things that don't feel like down time to them during that time. The partner who can do inductive reasoning may need to plan to take the children as soon as he or she gets home to give the partner with IRI down time to recover from the day, especially if he or she is an introvert.

It will be really important to plan this out so that each partner gets what he or she needs. The partner who has IRI may need to have his or her needs met first in order to manage the other family needs well. Make sure partners negotiate this.

It may help to have a routine set up for this as far as the order of interaction. Understand that the time for each task or person may vary some, so try to be a little flexible. Parents with IRI may get overloaded in working out partner or family issues. You may have to stop before things are resolved and give them some processing time or come back to the issue the next day. It may help to have down time between each family-related issue that needs addressing. *Planning* for these types of things can help the marriage and family tremendously. If you get stuck, don't wait until you are so frustrated you can't stand it. Find a psychotherapist that understands IRI and get the help you need right away. You deserve it!

Down Time

To help those with IRI, understand down time is crucial for them. Families need to plan for that for children. Don't keep them too busy. Give them slots of time that aren't planned where they can choose their activity and/or choose to be by themselves. Parents who have IRI need to negotiate and plan with their partner for down time. Partners need to pay attention to when their partner with IRI is getting overloaded and take over parenting for a while. Learn when to interact with those with IRI and when to leave them alone.

For those with IRI, plan for down time and ask for it when you really need it. Find things in your down time that help you relax. Playing games, reading, listening to music, doing art, etc. are all good for letting your brain rest from all the Thinking when you struggle with IRI.

Communication

It's important to learn to be specific when communicating and give all the information that is needed for those with IRI to understand. No one is used to communicating like that. We didn't learn that in our family growing up. We all assume that others think, feel, and have the same beliefs, expectations, etc. as we do. And we assume that others will come to the same conclusions on things that we do. Most of us are fairly close fairly often. But we all make mistakes and need clarification about things. The reality is that we are all unique. We all grew up in different families and cultures with different meanings to things. Even siblings in the same family have different perceptions. And we are all wired a little differently. *If we come to each person understanding that each of us is different, then we will have more grace in our attempts to understand each other.*

Those with IRI need to be taught social skills. There are some similar things, which fall under general social rules, like how close we stand to someone when we talk with a person. In some cultures, we need to keep eye contact while communicating; in other cultures, it is rude. We all need to adapt to the culture we are living in. Those with IRI need help to understand the cultural expectations, as well as the family expectations. *They need direct, specific information about how to communicate and when,* or they may fail in social interactions. Parents and teachers need to tell children specific expectations of behavior, why they have those expectations, and how to do the behavior, so that children who have IRI will learn to interact appropriately. Many times, they aren't given enough information or specific enough information to meet the expectations. And often they need information about how to cope with their own feelings in those situations while they are trying to meet the expectations of others. (See the section on "Stress, Worry, Fear, Anxiety, and Panic" on page 98 for help with this issue.)

In order for those with IRI to answer questions, it's important for us to ask for the information we really want. (Remember the "Making Meaning" section where the slight change in words affected how they understood the question?) People often ask general questions—why does this happen or why did she do that—and assume others will know what information they are seeking. Sometimes people are looking for the motivation behind the behavior. Sometimes they are looking for the feelings that prompted the behavior. Sometimes they want to know the situation that prompted the behavior. Often people get very defensive if asked a why question because they assume it is an attack, a judgment about their choice of response. Most people will attempt to respond without asking for more clarification about what the person really wants to know. Those with IRI will not ask for clarification unless they are taught to do so and how to do it. Miscommunication happens all the time, and interpretations of motives are often wrong among all of us. *The more you can slow down the communication and hold your feeling response until you know what the other person is thinking, the more successful the communication will be for everyone.*

It's important to learn to ask the question you have in mind and then rethink what you are actually wanting to find out. Then reword your question, being as specific as you can be to the answer you are seeking. This will help those with IRI access the information (remember the warehouse analogy?). You will need to practice this regularly. It took me a long time to write this book. I had to keep going over it and refining what I said and how I said it so that adults who have IRI could read this book and understand what I am saying. This was great practice for thinking in ways that allow for good communication with those who have IRI. Reading and rereading this book can help you in your thinking and communication as well.

It is important to ask those with IRI what they understand you are asking or requesting. Don't ask them *if* they understand; instead, ask them *what* they understand. Having them tell you is good practice for them to think through requests and to formulate their own thinking about it. Don't accept a word-for-word repeat of what you asked unless the request is very short and very clear. Instead, ask them again what they understand you are asking. Their answer will help you to determine if they have the right instructions to respond or complete a task. This will also allow those with IRI to be more successful in responding or doing the task. You will learn more about how they think when a request is made. This helps you to know where they typically go in their thinking. That helps you to form better questions or requests in the future. Then you can coach them on how most people think and what most people are asking when they make a request like yours. That way they will be more successful in social situations.

Communication

To help those with IRI, remember they need to understand the cultural expectations as well as the family expectations. *They need direct, specific information about how to communicate and when,* or they may fail in social interactions. Parents and teachers need to tell children specific expectations of behavior, why we have them, and how to do the behavior in order for children who have IRI to learn to interact appropriately. Many times, they aren't given enough information or specific enough information to meet the expectations.

It is important to ask those with IRI what they understand you are asking or requesting. Don't ask them *if* they understand; ask them *what* they understand. Having them tell you is good practice for them. And you can determine if they have the right instructions to respond or complete a task. It is good practice for them and a good habit to build in their daily life.

For those with IRI, learn to ask questions if there is something you don't understand. This should be done for important directions on things. You can't ask this all the time. Learn to know when to ask those questions so you are socially appropriate. Learn to share what you think you understand and ask if that is what the other person is meaning or wanting. We all misinterpret things. Asking for clarification can help avoid that. If people get upset, apologize. Then tell them what you understood them to want and ask if that was correct. Ask them for more information. This tells them that you were not trying to be hurtful; you just didn't understand. That helps heal the hurt in the relationship.

Colloquialisms and Idioms

The speech therapist may tell you that your child has a problem with understanding these. If you are like me, you will wonder what in the world they mean. I had to look them up in the dictionary for the exact definition. A colloquialism is an informal way of talking that usually does not make literal sense, but people usually understand what it really means. An idiom is an expression which when understood as a whole has a meaning that is different from the joined meaning of the parts.

An idiom or colloquialism is really a saying. They are used like shorthand in the general population to help explain something more simply or quickly. Let me give you some examples. I think about some of the sayings that have come into use over the years among teens like "rad," which stands for radical and was used when something was really positive or you liked it a lot. (It has gone out of style now.) "My bad" would really confuse those from other cultures and languages. It means "my mistake; I did that wrong." It doesn't mean that the person speaking is bad.

Just think of the text language that has come into being, like LOL (laugh out loud) or OMG. (You get to look that one up if you don't know it. Type in text dictionary in your computer's search engine, and you will get several options for looking up text language.) If you are older and just learning you have IRI, you may be totally lost in text language.

Idioms or colloquialisms can really confuse a person with IRI until they are explained. We have to catch ourselves when we use them and then offer another way of saying what we want to say that is simple, clear, and without extra meanings. It's also best to ask those with IRI what they think you mean by what you said. That way you can check if they are interpreting correctly.

> **Colloquialisms and Idioms**
>
> A colloquialism is a form of speech that is used in ordinary conversation that is informal, and an idiom is an expression that when understood as a whole has a meaning that is different from the joined meaning of the parts. They are used like shorthand in the general population to help explain something more simply or quickly.
>
> *To help those with IRI,* you will need to avoid colloquialisms and idioms or explain these sayings when you use them in talking or writing. Those with IRI will often not understand such expressions. You also may have to ask the person with IRI to tell you what he or she thinks you meant to make sure the person is understanding things correctly.
>
> *For those with IRI,* if people say something that you don't understand, ask them what they mean. If you are older and don't want to stand out, try to remember it or write it down and do an Internet search or ask your parents or partner. You need to understand what others are saying and not be left out.

Sensory Issues

A diagnosis of SID (sensory integration disorder) can occur with those who have IRI. It can occur for highly sensitive people and others in general. It often isn't diagnosed at all. People just assume that's the way they are. Understanding what is happening is important and learning to cope a must.

Sensory Overload or Lack of Filters

When our brain develops in the womb and through the first year of life, pathways are set for seeing, hearing, touching, tasting, and smelling. A whole variety of things in our body develop, including many reflexes. Our reflexes need to be developed, integrated, and most turned off until we need them. Almost everyone has his or her reflexes developed. If you have them developed but not integrated, you will struggle with feeling connected to your body and being able to move your body well and with coordination. You won't be able to skip and sing at the same time. Or you will physically struggle to say what you are thinking because those pathways are not connected well, etc. So we need them integrated. We also need to turn off most of them, or we have something like ADHD where we are constantly scanning the environment for danger, feeling endangered, and needing to move because of it and not being able to be still and focus on anything outside of scanning.

For some people, including many of those on the autism spectrum, their brain pathways were affected in development so they often have higher sensitivity in one or all of their five senses. *They have to find a way to cope with being overloaded by their senses all the time.* They may avoid crowds, flashing lights, loud noises, foods/restaurants, or anywhere they experience the overload in any of their five senses.

Educational and developmental kinesiology can often help with some sensory issues. Carol Kranowitz has written several *Out of Sync* books that can be very helpful with sensory issues. Dealing with electromagnetic frequency (EMF) and radio frequency (RF) in the home can also help. The correct nutrition and sleep are very important. See "Resources" for more information.

Sound

For some when they hear loud sounds, it may trigger all sound tones at the same time in their brain, and they are overloaded with sound. Or the loudness may have no filter so that when the volume increases, their pain increases. These people will cover their ears and cringe around fire bells, fire engines, airplanes, etc. It can be physically painful. If they hear themselves with sensitivity, then they may talk very quietly to avoid overloading themselves. If they are hyper-sensitive to sound, they may interpret your talking with them as your yelling at them. *And it may not even feel or sound like yelling to you.*

If you can lower your voice to meet them in their comfort zone, they will hear you better. Otherwise, they will be managing the yelling they perceive instead of what you are trying to say. It's important to let them know you were not yelling, the level at which you were talking, perhaps the feeling you were meaning to convey, and that they were being sensitive at that time (with no criticism since they couldn't control their sensitivity). They need that feedback. Consider carrying ear plugs with you at all times if you have sound sensitivity. I have since high school and use them regularly.

The difficulty for parents, teachers, and bosses is that *those who have filter issues may not be able to filter out if you yell at someone else.* It will cause pain and anxiety for them. *If you yell at them, they will usually be overloaded.* Trying to manage the overload will keep them from hearing a word you say—which is true for most of us. In either case, they will want to leave, hide, avoid, even if the reason for yelling is relatively appropriate or not directed at them.

If they can't hear themselves, they may yell at you and not realize they are yelling. It's important to give them that feedback and have them practice for the correct level of sound. They may or may not be able to adjust the volume.

And if you have someone with both, the person will be sensitive to your raised voice but not notice his or her own raised voice. Getting a tool that measures the sound level and having the person watch it while talking may help the individual begin to feel a difference if he or she can't hear at what level he or she is talking.

Touch

Those who are sensitive to touch often can't handle clothing tags, types of material, certain ways in which clothing is sewn together, etc. You may think they are just being picky, but the reality is that *they are again overloaded by feeling the material/tag all the time. They can't filter it out or ignore it.* So it will be important to remove tags and buy the clothing in material that does not overwhelm or distract them.

This can be one reason for a colicky baby or a child that doesn't want to be cuddled or held. It may not be an attachment issue but a sensitivity issue. Gently rubbing a baby with various materials and noting his or her response can tell you whether it's touch or not and what is calming or triggering. You can then avoid those things that trigger crying or a negative reaction.

Smell/Taste/Texture

Those with sensitivity to smell will be overloaded by someone's perfume/cologne, deodorant, or foods. They will avoid public places in order to manage the overload they smell. They again can't filter or block it out as most of us do once we identify the smell. They will also struggle with eating because *taste is affected by smell, and they can overload in both areas at the same time.*

Know that children usually have more sensitive taste and smell and won't like as much spice as older folks. And the older you get, the less sensitive your senses are so you need/want more. But for those with smell/taste sensitivities, you really have to be patient about the limited foods that they like. *It's not just what they like but also what won't overload them.*

Or it may be a texture issue. Some people react more intensely to certain textures in the mouth. They will spit out food because the texture is squishy or grainy or stringy. And they will refuse to eat it in the future, even though the taste is not a problem. You may be able to change the texture through mashing, pureeing, cooking, or cutting it if they like the taste. Be sure to ask them what they experience so you know if it's the smell, taste, or texture that is the problem.

Visual

People who struggle with visual overload will often avoid looking around or at people. *They become overwhelmed by the amount of information that comes in visually. This can be either/both an inductive reasoning difficulty or a visual overload issue.* To demand that these folks look you in the eye is really demanding that they be OK with being overwhelmed. They will never be OK with information overload, but they can learn to look at you. They often have a very blank expression with wide open eyes where they have learned to withdraw inside themselves in order to cope. Or they may squint to shut down information.

Those with IRI and sensory overload will have an even harder time because they have one more thing they have to manage. On top of figuring out each and every person and situation, they will be managing their senses. These folks may be more withdrawn in social situations because of that.

I knew one person who saw everything that others saw but overlaid on top of that was a constantly changing color pixilation. He was coping with that all the time and tended not to use his visual field enough and ran into things. He thought everyone saw that way until he hit his teens and then realized that wasn't typical. It did go away as he got older and changed his nutrition.

Working with someone who knows Brain Gym/educational kinesiology, cranial-sacral work, energy medicine, sensory integration therapy, or visceral manipulation and structural integration (by someone careful) can help. Carol Kranowitz has written several *Out of Sync* books can be very helpful with sensory issues. You have to come at sensory overload through the physical realm. Again, helping those with sensory overload with the anxiety this causes will be very helpful if they are open to working on it.

Sensory Overload or Lack of Filters

To help those with IRI, be aware that many of them have sensory sensitivities or lack filters. It's important to identify the sensitivities and help them manage them as well as possible. There are several modalities can than lessen the intensity or even clear the sensitivity.

For those with IRI, you need to learn what is overwhelming for you and the ways to manage what overwhelms you. Then you need to plan for situations that are overwhelming and do the strategies you have learned.

Over-stimulating Environments

I can't tell you how many times parents get frustrated because people do not understand that those who have IRI can't relax in any situation that is new or when there are multiple people involved. People will tell those with IRI to relax or not to worry or try to reassure them, but it won't work because they don't understand what is causing the anxiety. Have you ever been able to relax when you were really tense or anxious and someone told you to just relax? Often reassuring students will not work. Period. They have to get out of the over-stimulating environment. If they have to do a presentation at school or work, they need to have a time to prepare beforehand in a non-stimulating environment and then to calm down afterwards. I don't know any public school that allows for that, and in general, I know hardly anyone that really understands why he or she needs it.

There are often times where students or adults have to present in front of a group by themselves or as part of a small group. In working in small groups, students with IRI will often do more of the behind-the-scenes preparation work while others from the small group present—unless those with IRI are forced to present. Students with IRI usually do better if they have to present only to one or two people they know so they can focus on the presentation and not on the over-stimulating environment.

You can explore how to limit input while they are presenting in order to lower anxiety. For example:

- Visit the place of presentation ahead of time and determine focal points to use during the presentation.
- Look over a person's head and focus on a point or two (to not look fixed) or a point over each section of the audience while presenting.
- Focus on the slides they are presenting with only occasional glances at the audience at predetermined points.
- Learn to move to points where they should look, based on the slides they are covering so they don't look fixed.
- If they are talking with an individual, look between the person's eyebrows instead of at the eyes or only focus on one eye (which is what we all generally do).

Teach those with IRI the definition of worry, fear, anxiety, and panic. Help them determine which category fits for the moment or the situation they are struggling with. Have them rate it on a scale of zero to four, and have them develop a list of coping strategies that work for them.

The greatest fear that most people have is talking in front of groups. I've had that fear most of my life, and I've done hundreds of presentations of various kinds. I've tried all kinds of ways to get rid of it. I tried exposure therapy by speaking about twenty-five times in one year to see if that would change things. All it made me feel was tired. I have significantly lowered my fear by using energy psychology, educational kinesiology, energy medicine, and clearing pre- and pari-natal shock and trauma. I've also worked with a couple of body workers that do visceral manipulation, cranial-sacral work, and structural integration. I encourage you all to figure out your triggers and find ways to clear them if you can. For those with IRI, learn to cope first and then try some of these modalities to see if anything can help.

Color

Have those with IRI look at color swatches and tell you what makes them feel calm or relaxed, happy, neutral, tense, etc. You may have to explain what each of those terms mean and the physical sensations that match the words if they struggle to make meaning and aren't very in touch with their body. Then paint a space for relaxation with the color that helps them. Or drape fabric in the area. If they struggle to wake up, check to see if a color helps them wake up or be more energetic and use it. Most of us wake with blue light (like the morning sky) and become sleepy with yellow light (sunset). If they tend towards depression, find a color that makes them feel happier and use it in many locations.

Sound

Find out their level of sensitivity by slowly turning the volume up from very low and having them tell you when they experience loud. Then have them tell you when it hurts their ears. Find the volume that makes them most comfortable. This helps you know how loud to speak and what to avoid. Try different types of music and find out which ones help them relax or feel happy.

Taste

Give those with IRI different foods and have them tell you what they taste and how strong the taste is based on a zero-to-four scale if they struggle to rate things or on a hundred-point scale if they can do it easily and like to be more specific. Taste each food yourself so you know how strong it is for you. That way you know their level in comparison to what you experience. Find the level of taste that is not overwhelming to them. Often those with taste sensitivity will eat very bland foods, like rice, white bread, etc., because it is not stimulating. This can change as people age because our body loses sensitivity as we grow older. Having good nutrition can also help change this aspect.

Texture

Those with IRI can have a high sensitivity to textures of clothing and foods. Some people can't handle squishy-feeling things or grainy things. Energy psychology, educational kinesiology, and sensory integration can all be helpful. Some people believe that exposure therapy helps, and it may when people are young and their brain is still developing. It may be helpful to those who are highly motivated to make change in this area. Otherwise, it can just be overwhelming and not helpful.

Temperature

Those with IRI can be sensitivity to warm or cold. Some bodies adjust more easily or quickly to temperature changes. Those with sympathetic shock (fight or flight is on) will often be too warm, and those with parasympathetic shock (pretend you are dead) will often be too cold. Those with thyroid issues (who generally have shock issues) will also struggle to adjust to temperatures. Dress in ways that allow for removing or adding clothing that will keep you comfortable. See a therapist that knows about shock and how to clear it, and your system may change. Nutrition is often a part of this issue. Seeing a naturopath or nutritionist can be helpful.

Over-stimulating Environments

To help those with IRI, explore what can lower stimulation for them in the environment, including color, sound, texture, taste, and temperature.

For those with IRI, color, sound, texture, taste, and temperature may all have impacts on you, and you may not be aware of it. Take time to note if any of these are helpful or over-stimulating to you. Ask those close to you to notice if you have reactions and tell you. You can always lower the stimulation by changing your environment. There is help to desensitize some things using Brain Gym/educational kinesiology, cranial-sacral work, energy medicine, sensory integration therapy, or visceral manipulation and structural integration (by someone careful).

Listening to Those with Sensory Overload

It's vitally important to listen to those who have sensory overload and attempt to accommodate them or help them accommodate when you can. Do not discount their pain, irritation, or difficulty ignoring the stimulation. They have no control of it. Some children respond very violently to the information overload to try to protect themselves. They need to be taught other options and to use words as they grow older. They may not be able to easily tell you what is happening if they have IRI, especially if they are very young. They may appear as colicky babies so you have to pay close attention to stimulants of all kinds. Or babies may go to sleep when overloaded. Pay attention to their sleep patterns. Do they nap in groups even though they haven't been overly stimulated and it is not their nap time? If that happens regularly, then they are on overload. When they are old enough to cover ears or eyes, pull at clothing tags or clothes, etc. you will be able to tell more quickly. Identifying what is going on is vitally important. *Understand that they don't have control of their senses the way most people do. Helping them find ways to cope is necessary.* Let them know appropriate behavior and ways to manage their sensitivity and expect them to do it at age-appropriate levels. Otherwise, give them ways to leave the situation that are appropriate for their age.

A reaction to sensory overload by those with IRI can look like anxiety, obsessive compulsive disorder, reactive attachment disorder or social phobias. But it is not based on an emotional response; is it based on physical discomfort. Again, you have to ask the right questions to know what's really going on. Don't assume it is emotional if you are a counselor. Ask questions that address both the emotional and the physical reactions at the time of and after any event where they are triggered. Did anything frighten them? What frightened them? Has that happened in the past? Do they fear it in the future? Is something physically uncomfortable or painful? Are they so distracted that they can't pay attention to anything but what is bothering them? How often do they experience the discomfort or pain? How long did they experience it? If there is a pattern, search out what the trigger is both physically and emotionally so you know what help they need. Otherwise, you will miss a large piece, and they will continue to struggle, with neither of you knowing what is causing that issue.

Parents/family will have to grieve that their child has this issue and how it affects the entire family. And get support to let go of your expectations that they overcome this. Then you will be open to whatever change occurs over time with whatever help is chosen, and you will feel gratitude for the change. See the section on "Grief" in "Resources."

Sensory sensitivity can be difficult when there isn't an external way to mediate the problem. You have to work at it through the physical realm. Working with someone who knows Brain Gym/educational kinesiology, energy medicine, cranial-sacral work, sensory integration therapy or visceral manipulation and structural integration (by someone careful) can help. Google each, and you will get more information, as well as practitioners in your area. Some chiropractors, naturopaths, occupational therapists, and massage therapists do cranial-sacral work and/or visceral manipulation and structural integration. Carol Kranowitz has written several *Out of Sync* books that can be very helpful with sensory issues.

Listening to Those with Sensory Overload

To help those with IRI who have sensory sensitivities, realize they do not have control of these sensitivities. It's important to accept them and help these individuals cope well with them. Those with IRI may be able to reduce their sensitivities with the proper help or nutrition.

For those with IRI, seek help for your sensitivities. Most people don't have them, and you can learn to change some of them and manage the rest.

Other Sensory Issues

Under-Responsivity is when people feel a lack of stimulation even when the touch is intense or hurtful. They may need longer stimulation, more frequent stimulation or more intense stimulation to feel the same level that most people feel. They will often not react much to getting cut or bruised. They may chew on inedible objects like clothing or erasers. They may tire easily. This can be common in those with autism. Those with IRI might not be paying attention to their body, but once reminded they can access what is happening to them. They may need help with figuring out levels of intensity or the right words to describe what they feel.

Sensory Seeker will crave stimulation - orally by chewing gum or sucking on their clothes, have the TV volume or music volume on high, find things to touch all the time, fidget or find it impossible to sit still. Those with autism can have this. This can be a way to cope with under-responsivity, is a way to manage anxiety or can be part of ADHD.

Combinations can happen depending on the senses involved. One may have sensory sensitivity to sound and under-responsivity to touch.

Sensory Discrimination is the difficulty with telling the difference between various stimulants. Those that have this may not know they are touching something unless they can see themselves touching it or not be aware of the heat of a pot of soup boiling until they can smell the cooking. They may not hear the difference in sounds like will and still. They may struggle to discriminate between identifying the taste vs the texture of foods. This is common in those with autism. Their brain has not wired things up or they can't figure out which sense is happening in response to what stimulus.

Postural Disorders happen when people have poor muscle tone. They may struggle to zip up their pants or hold a pencil to write. They may have difficulty sitting up straight or even staying in their seat without falling out of it. They often feel fatigued. Again this is common with autism.

Dyspraxia occurs when a person has difficulty imagining, coordinating and then executing movement. It can involve large muscles (gross-motor,) fine muscles (fine-motor,) or oral-motor skills or a combination of them. These folks seem clumsy, trip or bump into people a lot. They may struggle to hold a crayon or pen to write. They may struggle to chew or eat or tend to drool. Again, this is common with autism. Those with IRI may bump into people if they are focusing elsewhere at the time.

An occupational therapist (OT) who works with sensory issues can help to evaluate what the difficulties are with senses and what to do to address them. Those with IRI may have none of these or some of these. If you suspect any of them are a problem, please see an OT trained in sensory issues and get an evaluation done. There are books in the resource section that can help with sensory issues.

Highly Sensitive People vs. Inductive Reasoning Issues

Some people are born more sensitive in a variety of ways and not just the five senses. These highly sensitive people often have sensory sensitivities, but they can do inductive reasoning, perhaps even better than most. A highly sensitive person can be so attuned to others that it's as if he or she can read other people's mind. This can be true with people that are close to the individual or with all the people he or she is around. The highly sensitive person may be too caring or more impacted by others' feelings than others who can do inductive reasoning. The person will take care of others to lower their pain, stress, and tension that he or she feels from others. This is really self-care for the individual and not co-dependency. The person can also be more sensitive to the environment around him or her, for instance, feel the need a plant has for water or the health issues of a pet. Such a person often feels overwhelmed by others or by the environment and has to learn to manage this sensitivity. Learning grounding and shielding can help. See my website, www.Counsel-Heal.com, for instructions. Check out Elaine Aron's website and books for more information at www.hsperson.com. Working with someone doing educational or developmental kinesiology or energy medicine can really help.

A person with IRI can be totally unaware of what is going on with others or how his or her behavior impacts others. The person with IRI won't pick up body cues or vocal cues or sense the mood in a room. The individual may be highly sensitive in the five senses but not to others.

Highly Sensitive People vs. Inductive Reasoning Issues
Highly sensitive people often have sensory sensitivities, but they can do inductive reasoning, perhaps even better than most. They can be so attuned to you that it's as if they read your mind. They need to learn to set good boundaries relationally and energetically to have good relationships. Those with IRI may be highly sensitive in their five senses but not to others. They will struggle with empathy.

Sixth Sense and Safety

Our sixth sense is our brain's ability to note very specific behavior, attach meaning to it, and make sense of it in the larger context. We see someone, and we feel afraid, but we don't know why. Some part of our brain has logged information and correlates it to the fact that past experience tells us this type of person is not safe. We don't get it on a Thinking level; we get it in our gut. Those with IR issues can't do cross referencing or making these connections on an everyday level. They struggle constantly to make meaning about what they see, hear, touch, taste, and feel. There is no sixth sense for them. So they will generally not pick up that someone is not safe. You have to teach children rules about who is safe to talk to and to be around and what information is safe to share verbally, on the Internet, over the phone, etc.

Sixth Sense and Safety
To help those with IRI, understand that they will not sense danger from others well. They will either be so stressed that they miss it, or they will miss the body cues. Be sure to teach them what to look for in behavior from people who will likely want to hurt them. I know that none of us really wants to face this, but if we want our children to stay safe, we need to address this directly and with good information.

For those with IRI, there are a few people in the world that do like to hurt other people. You need to learn the behaviors they display and what you do in order to keep yourself safe. All kids need to learn about this, but you need more specific information. Ask your parents, grandparents, psychotherapist, or pastor for this information.

Chapter 3 | Additional Health Issues That Impact Those with IRI

What Causes IRI, Autism, Asperger's Syndrome, Social Communication Disorder, and ADD?

Whenever I talk with parents or present to professionals, I always get this question. There is no clear answer to it. Our brain is a very complex and sensitive system. There is a lot of research happening now, and we are in the beginning stages of understanding how our brain works. What we do know is that the brain is very flexible and will make connections as genetics and experience affect it. No two brains are exactly alike. If there is a greater need for something, then our brain will adapt and create space for that learning. If we have a major interest, our brain will make room and wire for that. If we don't use something, our brain will slowly let go of the connections to that information, and it will become more difficult to retrieve that information over time.

I do have beliefs about factors that affect brain function. There are several possible issues involved in why people have IRI, including genetics, brain trauma, sleep issues, vision issues, nutrition, toxicity, and EMF/RF.

Genetics

Genetics play a part in how our brain is wired. From those I've talked to in the field and what I've read, there is clear evidence that many genes have on and off switches. We may have a predisposition to any number of things, but what we are exposed to in our environment will determine what is on and what is off in our genes. This includes experiences. The way we think about things in our life leads us to various feelings that release the hormones related to those feelings. Chemicals, including hormones, are how our brain speaks to itself, and they affect how our brain functions. So where the mind goes, energy flows—good or bad for us. How you think has a major impact on how your brain functions.

Brain Trauma

It is estimated that the brain has a billion neurons, and each has thousands of connections. It is an amazingly alive and complex system, and we are each wired a little differently. The more I've learned about the brain through the years, the more respect and care I have for my body and brain.

Brain trauma can be caused by many things, including birth (the structure of the mother's pelvis, cord wrapped around the neck at birth, the use of forceps, etc.), falling or rising suddenly and hitting your head, being hit in the head by others or shaken (accidental or abuse), car accidents, sports accidents (football, soccer, baseball, hockey, etc.), lack of oxygen due a stroke, heart attack, or sleep apnea, etc.

Many people don't think of being knocked down in football or hit in the head with a soccer ball as brain trauma, but it can be. Your brain is actually fairly soft, like a stick of butter, and when it stops suddenly, it impacts the skull and the bones that hold it in place. You feel stunned and as if you can't think clearly for a few moments. Or if the trauma is greater, you may find your brain not working well in some ways for a much longer period of time. Sometimes symptoms show up and slowly improve over six months to a year. For children, sometimes symptoms may not show up for a year or two until the next developmental stage is reached. By then, most people have forgotten the trauma and don't know what is causing the issues that are seen. You may have a major trauma like a stroke, which has significant lasting effects. Your brain can heal some as the blood overflow is removed by your system, but some areas may never work again, and you will have to relearn skills using other areas of your brain.

When I first started working as a therapist, I worked with those who had a stroke or head injury in a post hospital rehab program. Doctors used to think that you only had so many brain cells. If any were damaged or killed, you lost function and never recovered it. So they would tell these folks that they would never recover. Yet we saw patients continue to change and improve during the one to three years in our program. That led me to a lifetime of studying about the brain and therapy models that address how the brain is wired. We can change our brains in a variety of natural ways, including changing our thinking, feelings, nutrition, and exercise and through the use of mind and body modalities.

Our brain is very flexible in its wiring. There are people who are changing their brain. Barbara Arrowsmith Young developed a whole program for herself that is now used in her schools. The book, *The Brain That Changes Itself* by Norman Doidge, shares stories of a number of scientists who are helping people basically to rewire their brains—people with issues from autism to inner ear and balance issues to love hormone addictions, etc. It is a very interesting book to read, and it is encouraging. He has another book out called, *The Brain's Way of Healing,* which has additional information.

Back in the 1980s, a group started in the greater Seattle, Washington, area to support those with head injuries because many experienced personality changes or changes in function, and most people just didn't believe it. Now we have fMRI and SPECT scans that can show how the brain is firing and if there are any areas in the brain that aren't functioning well. Our understanding of the brain is expanding immensely.

Sleep Issues

Most of us have issues with sleep at times in our life. Lack of sleep is one of the main reasons for ill health. You may have trouble falling asleep due to anxiety, stress, the blue lighting of computer screens, phones or TV, eating too late or using a stimulant like coffee or nicotine too soon before bed, etc. Some people struggle to stay asleep due to hormone imbalances, the neighbor's dog, having to use the restroom, etc. Or you may wake early due to hormone imbalances, light, partner snoring, etc. Or you may sleep too much, which can be a symptom of depression or other hormone imbalances. You may be working out a lot of things in your dream time. Often when people begin to work on things in their waking time, they begin to sleep better because they aren't working on those things in their sleep time.

It may be that your hormones are affecting your sleep patterns. When we have a lot of stress, it can affect our cortisol levels, which regulate waking and sleeping. I think most teens struggle with hormones and cortisol levels. It may be menopausal changes for women. Getting blood tests to check various levels can help you determine if you have deficiencies that might be making you tired. (See "Nutrition" on page 151.) Taking some supplements, like Melatonin, Seraphos, Cortrex, Calms Forte (homeopathic), or sleep medications can help. Be sure to check with your MD or ND to determine what might help you the most and the dosages. You need to make sure that what you choose to take will not have negative effects or combine in a negative way with medications or supplements you are already taking.

If your blood work looks good and you sleep a regular schedule but are still tired on waking, it may be appropriate to have a sleep study done through your physician or neurologist to determine if you are truly sleeping through the night or not. Sometimes people don't breathe well through the night and wake up to various degrees. You may not be aware of waking. It is called sleep apnea. You may not breathe well at night because of your body structure (a large soft palate, a large lower jaw) or because you are overweight and the weight shuts down the airways when you lie down. Your back, neck, or jaw may be out of alignment and cause restriction. It can help to see a chiropractor or someone who does visceral manipulation and structural integration when you have structural issues. CPAP or APAP machines or dental retainers (always with exercises to release your jaw in the morning) can help you to breathe better and therefore sleep better at night. If you have a high palate, you can work with an orthodontist to spread your palate and correct for bite in ways that can also open up the breathing passage.

Vision Issues

When the eyes see clearly but are not working together, it can cause symptoms that look like ADD, including short attention span, distractibility, disorganization, procrastination, and difficulties with forethought, judgment, and impulse control. *You can't focus when your eyes can't focus and work together.* This can be caused by birth trauma, brain trauma, toxicity, or genetic issues. You can get help using kinesiology, vision therapy, cranial-sacral work, or visceral manipulation and structural integration. There are some optometrists and ophthalmologists who diagnose and treat people using vision therapy. See "Resources" for more information.

Nutrition

This is a significant issue for everyone. Our body needs to get enough of the right foods to help our brain and body function well. We have to have enough clean air and water, nutritious foods without toxins, and good digestion for our body and brain to be nourished well. The following are the things I have found through the years in healing myself and helping others to heal that appear to be foundations for health.

Keep the pH of your body alkaline.

This means eating more vegetables and some fruit, some meat or legumes, and limited grains. The book that I like the best is *The Ultimate pH Solution* by Michelle Schoffro Cook. We generally think if the food is acidic then that's what causes our body to be acidic. That is not true. We need to look at what the body needs in order to break down the food. Meat requires more acid to break it down; therefore our body will create an acidic environment in our digestion system to break it down. Citrus has plenty of acid in it so it breaks down more easily, and our body doesn't need to create a lot more acid to break it down. Many diseases cannot exist in an alkaline environment so we will generally be healthier if our body is more alkaline.

Eat according to your blood type.

The book *Eat Right for Your Type* by Peter J. D'Adamo explains a lot about how different blood types process food. He has food lists that can be helpful. Your body may not tolerate some foods well and have things like indigestion, but you may not have allergic reactions. I found the explanations about how the body processes certain foods fit me exactly. I had spent ten years figuring it out on my own. If only the book had come out sooner!

Eat only organic, and eat free-range and grass-fed meats.

Your body will have fewer toxins from pesticides, herbicides, antibiotics, and growth hormones to deal with. We have enough psychological stress in our culture; we don't need to add those physical stressors as well.

I understand that those on limited incomes will struggle with this so priorities can go in this order—organic dairy, avoid the dirty dozen (or now fifteen) fruits and vegetables (search for the latest list), organic fruits and vegetables, organic grains, wild-caught fish, organic free-range meats, and last is organic, grass-fed meats. Buy local and fresh if you can. Grocery stores will gas, radiate, and store many fruits and vegetables for up to a year, and they lose their nutritional value before they enter the store.

Make your own meals.

Store-bought prepared foods do not have to list all the chemicals they use to prepare their foods. They can add whatever flavors they want, including ones that trick your brain into thinking that something is ripe and ready to eat when they got the cheapest, perhaps least ripe product with limited nutrition and added the flavorings. Assume you are getting little nutritional value and a lot of filler. Read the book *Non-Toxic, Natural and Earthwise* by Debra Lynn Dadd. The single best investment our family made early on was buying a freezer. When I cook, I make a lot, and it doesn't take me that much extra time. I freeze additional meals and defrost one when I'm busy.

Check your nutritional levels.

Have blood work done yearly that includes a complete blood count (CBC), which can show certain blood levels, as well as if you have an infection. Have your ferritin level checked, which shows how your body is utilizing iron (most of us are actually anemic because the CBC level tests what's in our body not how our body is utilizing it). Have your serum zinc level and your vitamin D3 level checked. All these have major impacts on neurotransmitters and therefore on how our brain is functioning. Work with a DAN! (Defeat Autism Now) physician or a naturopath that focuses on nutrition.

Consider going gluten and dairy free (GFDF) if you have digestion problems or allergies.

It takes six months to a year to really clean up your digestive track once you go fully gluten free or dairy free. I took B vitamins for many, many years and found I didn't need them once I went GFDF and healed my digestive track. I used to take a lot of vitamins and minerals. Now I don't need them. Omega 3s and vitamin D are also natural antidepressants for many people. I have information on going GFDF on my website, www.Counsel-Heal.com.

Toxins

Toxicity exposure deposits things in our brain or body that affect our hormones, including additives in foods (companies are not required to list everything they put in a food because it's considered proprietary information), chemicals from industries now and in the past (remember the Superfund sites that they are still cleaning up?), pesticides, herbicides, and nanotechnology. (Nanoparticles are in all common cosmetics, some other substances we put on our skin, and some supplements. Manufacturers of those products aren't required to list those ingredients. And the manufacture of the products has no regulation or oversight, so we don't how nanoparticles are affecting us.) Our vaccinations contained mercury as a preservative for many years, and many still do contain mercury or aluminum. So beware your regular flu shot. It may be making you sick in a different way. All of which affect our body and brain health.

There are ways to clear toxins from your system. Working with a naturopath or a DAN! physician can be very helpful. There are a couple of books worth reading—*Children with Starving Brains* by Jacquelyn McCandless and Jack Zimmerman and *Non-Toxic, Natural and Earthwise* by Debra Lynn Dadd.

Cell Phones, Cell Tower Antennas, Wi-Fi, and Electromagnetic Frequencies

Radio frequencies (RF) and electromagnetic frequencies (EMF) may also play a part in why people have IRI or any number of diagnoses. RF and EMF cause the body to be stimulated to various degrees depending on the amount of time exposed and the intensity of exposure.

EMFs are emitted by anything that uses electricity, including our cell phones, iPads, iPods, TVs, computers, stoves, refrigerators, fans, lights, etc. Because they are small waves, they die out quickly, generally about a foot away from the item. But we hold our cell phone, our mouse, or touch our computer touch pad, Nook, stand by our refrigerator or stove, and expose our body to much more than we are aware of in our day-to-day life.

RFs are long waves that penetrate everything but a full metal box. These waves go through your body every day. We have always gotten some from the sun and the general universe, but we have increased the number immensely with Wi-Fi and cell phone use. All the cell phone antennas, cell towers, Wi-Fi units, and radio towers emit them.

There was a study done in Europe on worms. Worms reproduce themselves when broken in half. The researchers took a worm, broke it in half, allowed one to reproduce in a controlled environment, and it reproduced itself just fine. The other part they exposed to two hours of a cell phone on but not in use (which means less EMFs than when in use), and it could not reproduce itself. It became what they termed a monster worm whose DNA was significantly affected. That study changed my cell phone use significantly. You may want to read the book *Zapped* by Ann Louise Gittleman for more information. Consider a safer use of cell phones and electrical devices in your home. See my website, www.Counsel-Heal.com, for more information on this topic.

Smart meters have been placed by power companies (and aren't needed unless they plan to bill in the future according to what each appliance uses including TVs, stoves, refrigerators, computers, etc.), and they have been making people sick. Every state that has placed them has a group that is fighting them because so many people are getting sick. They put out a lot of RF throughout the home. People on the East Coast have been moving to the Appalachian Mountains to get away from them. Search the Internet for information on electrosmog. It's been a problem since the 1970s. Check my website, www.Counsel-Heal.com for more information on EMF and RF.

Chapter 4 | Diagnosing

The diagnostic manual developed out of the need to define behavior in the medical system. Therefore things are defined as disorders. I have yet to meet someone who doesn't have a diagnosis of one kind of disorder or another, so I don't think in those terms when I work with people. If you use insurance, you will have to receive a diagnosis in most cases. If you are the psychotherapist, you will have to give a diagnosis based on the client's behavior for that person to use his or her insurance. Don't let the diagnosis define who you are or who your client is, but let it organize what behaviors need to be changed.

There are levels of diagnoses depending on the number of behaviors and how long the person has experienced them. If the behavior stems from a reaction to a single particular trauma that's unresolved, it is called an adjustment disorder. If there have been multiple traumas that are unresolved and often intertwined, there will be a particular diagnosis or perhaps two depending on the behaviors displayed. If the behaviors are so constant that they only change when someone is on medication and the behaviors return when the medication is withdrawn, it is considered a personality disorder. Our continued growth in understanding the brain will continue to change the diagnostic criteria for different diagnoses and how to treat them.

What we are learning in the twenty-first century is how the brain is wired and what effects the wiring in the brain has on emotions and behavior. Those areas of the brain that fire together, wire together. So, if you had a trauma with a green car that is unresolved, then every green car may remind you of the trauma consciously or unconsciously. Once the trauma is resolved, green cars will no longer trigger the past trauma and the unresolved emotions attached to it.

The benefit and detriment of having IRI is that those connections are often not wired to other situations. So trauma in one situation (with the green car) will likely not get transferred to other situations (other green cars or any other car.) But the difficult side is that then those with IRI don't make connections between events or people or experiences and often don't transfer learning from old experiences to new ones unless they are taught to do it. *Educating those with IRI is the single most important tool in working with them. They need to understand in order to change their behavior, and they need tools and rules that they can apply to multiple situations. The tools and rules have to be direct, specific, and organized in a way that works for them.*

It can be difficult to determine a diagnosis because many people have aspects of more than one. I've seen people diagnosed one time with Asperger's, another time with ADD or ADHD, and another time with bipolar when they worked with different psychotherapists, psychologists, or psychiatrists. That can be confusing to family members. Social communication disorder is a step in the right direction to define what the social difficulty of Asperger's has been. The current three levels of autism diagnosis can be helpful for getting services but is pretty useless for understanding and working with those on the spectrum.

Inductive reasoning issues (IRI) can be seen in several diagnoses. Whether it is present depends on what areas of the brain are affected in the person. It is *the* reason for social communication disorder. Over the years I have seen IRI in those who had Asperger's, autism, ADD, ADHD, PDD-NOS, anxiety, social phobia, reactive attachment disorder, oppositional defiant disorder, obsessive compulsive disorder, bipolar, or narcissism diagnoses.

Diagnosing Inductive Reasoning Issues

I created the phrase "inductive reasoning issues" and determined how to use it. There is not a test for evaluating it at this time. Hopefully reading this book and filling out the worksheets will help you recognize when someone has or might have this issue. There are tools to evaluate social communication disorder. The difficulty lies in that Level 4s are often missed. You won't think they have a significant issue unless they are very Extroverted and you see it more often.

Signs of Inductive Reasoning Issues

Aspects can show up at any age. You will see many more things, especially in the early years for those at Level 3 and below. As they get older and more nuanced communication happens (fourth to fifth grade), IRI will also become more apparent. Their stress level will go up, and they will miss more social cues. Or else they will withdraw so others don't know they are missing social cues. They often scramble worse at puberty and struggle more with relationships then. So, IRI will often show up at that age for Level 4s.

Here are some of the behaviors that may indicate IRI from baby years on up.

- Intense focus on Dad's or Mom's face as a baby—parents may feel a sense of relief and not understand why they feel relief when their child moves to watching things in the world around six months
- Won't cry much as babies for food or changing or when they are sick
- Can be easily distracted from their body awareness
- Lack of pointing or gestures
- Lack of asking, "What's that?"
- Minimal or lack of facial expression
- Lack of eye contact with those outside the family

- Intently watches others play instead of joining in
- Does not color or do other work in preschool because he or she is watching peers
- No awareness of his or her own body in space and bumps into things, trips, etc.
- Struggles with fine motor skills like holding a fork, cutting with a knife, opening a jar, writing, etc. Uses large muscle groups (moving arm) instead of fingers
- Tends to be clumsy or have poor coordination
- Doesn't notice or know how to express when he or she is physically or emotionally hurt; may not cry
- Talks to himself or herself in playing alone or talks in a stream of consciousness
- Doesn't know how to use his or her imagination to play with objects
- May be able to do own imaginative play but not be able to join in imaginative play with others
- Tends to have one good friend or play with one friend at a time
- Is exhausted after playing with more than one person at a time or after coming home from school
- Not willing to be the center of attention (unless he or she is a fairly high extrovert)
- Mimics behavior, tones of voice, etc. of others, including TV characters
- Talks specifically (5:47, not a quarter to six) or with distinct enunciation
- Talks literally
- Lost in his or her own thoughts . . . and therefore
- Interrupts a lot

- Doesn't like things to change
- Wants to know the rules and what he or she is supposed to do
- Is very compliant when young
- Is seen as a rebel when older and the rules don't make sense, so he or she doesn't follow them
- But doesn't ask about the rules or ask to change the rules
- Doesn't like school (could be overwhelmed or bored)
- Doesn't ask others questions about themselves or other's opinions
- When asked, doesn't know what others may be experiencing
- Doesn't want to get rid of anything that is his or hers
- Is uncomfortable or fearful in new environments
- Doesn't understand humor
- Can't remember more than two or three instructions at a time
- Is disorganized
- Doesn't ask many or any questions
- Has a large vocabulary early
- Reads beyond grade level
- Wants to understand all possible aspects of something or someone
- Has an incredible memory, at least when young, or about a particular topic
- Notices all the details
- Is very honest, perhaps too much in some social situations
- Shares a lot of information or very little when asked
- Shares too many details and bores others or is socially inappropriate

- Has a high focus on one thing, possibly to the exclusion of other things or people
- Has a single high interest or maybe two; these may change periodically or stay the same thing over a long period of time
- Is intense
- Gets bored when required to focus on something other than his or her interest
- Learns the first time he or she sees or hears something *when young but can lose some of that in growing older and having so much to remember and figure out socially*
- Is often misunderstood by others and can't understand why
- Thinks and often talks beyond his or her peers
- Appears immature socially
- Expresses impatience or frustration that others can't follow or understand how they are thinking or what they are saying
- Doesn't feel as if he or she fits in anywhere

Those who have IRI will struggle with developing and using their verbal pragmatic abilities. They may struggle with being able to:

- Start, maintain, and end conversations appropriately
- Modify language depending upon the audience (peer, adult, teacher, etc.)
- Identify and express feelings, theirs and others
- Match the moods and emotions of their peers or those in the room
- Monitor and repair verbal interactions
- Monitor and adapt behavior to the situation

I've found that many with IRI struggle with the abstract thinking of algebra. And some are gifted in doing it. It seems to be one or the other.

Social Communication Disorder

Anyone with a diagnosis of social communication disorder has IRI and has difficulties with pragmatic language skills. American Speech-Language-Hearing Association has the largest list of evaluative tools with simple information on the year released, the age range, time and short description. There are a few that address more specific pragmatic language issues:

- Test of Pragmatic Language (TOPL)
- The Pragmatic Profile with the Clinical Evaluation of Language Fundamentals-IV (CELF-IV)
- Test of Problem Solving (TOPS)
- The Pragmatic Judgment subtest of the Comprehensive Assessment of Spoken Language (CASL)
- Pragmatic Language Skills Inventory (PLSI)
- Test of Narrative Language (TNL)
- Social Language Development Test (Published by Linguisystems, 2008)
- Social Skills Improvement Scale (SSIS)
- Orion's Pragmatic Language Skills (OPLS) Questionnaire

As of 2015, Michelle Garcia Winner has information about evaluating students in her book, *Me Thinking About You Thinking About Me.* She has developed the Social Thinking Dynamic Assessment Protocol and is developing an evaluation tool that will be much more specific about where students are in their social thinking ability.

Linguisystems has a relatively new tool with several aspects similar to Garcia Winner's. There are other tests that address focus, memory, attention, or organization issues. *If you think a client has IRI, the individual should be evaluated by someone who knows how to evaluate pragmatic language skills, or you can get educated yourself to administer the tests.* I currently think that no test is specific enough yet, but people will continue to develop more tests and tools to use.

Asperger's Syndrome or Autism

Asperger's syndrome is now diagnosed as autism. This change in the diagnostic manual was not helpful with regards to those with IRI. The tools used for diagnosing Asperger's may still be helpful in identifying issues related to IRI. Tests include:

Asperger Syndrome Diagnostic Scale (ASDS)
Autism Diagnostic Interview-Revised (ADI-R)
Autism Diagnostic Observation Schedule (ADOS)
Autism Screening Instrument for Educational Planning—Third Edition (ASIEP-3)
Childhood Autism Rating Scale (CARS)
Communication and Symbolic Behavior Scales Developmental Profile (CSBS DP)
Differential Assessment of Autism and Other Developmental Disorders (DAADD)
Gilliam Asperger's Disorder Scale (GADS)
Gilliam Autism Rating Scale, Second Edition (GARS-2)
Krug Asperger's Disorder Index (KADI)
Language Use Inventory (LUI)
Pervasive Developmental Disorders Screening Test-II (PDDST-II)
Psychoeduational Profile Revised (PEP-R)
Social Communication Questionnaire (SCQ)
Social Emotional Evaluation (SEE)
Social Responsiveness Scale (SRS)

Source for PDD Assessment and Intervention
Vineland Adaptive Behavior Scales, Second Edition (Vineland II)

Other Diagnostic Tools

Most people are familiar with IQ tests. Those who have IRI will tend to have really variable test scores within an area of testing. They will have higher-than-average, average, and lower-than-average results in the same section. This may give them an average to good overall score, but they will struggle in parts and often be even gifted in others. It is important to note the specifics and not pay attention to the overall scores. People have coined the term "twice exceptional" for gifted kids with learning disabilities.

IQ tests identify how people are doing in the following areas:

- Reading and writing skills
- Short-term memory—the ability to apprehend and hold information in immediate awareness, and then use it within a few seconds
- Long-term memory storage and retrieval—the ability to store information and fluently retrieve it later in the process of thinking
- Visual processing—the ability to perceive, analyze, synthesize, and think with visual patterns, including the ability to store and recall visual representations
- Auditory processing—the ability to analyze, synthesize, and discriminate auditory stimuli, including the ability to process and discriminate speech sounds that may be presented under distorted conditions
- Processing speed—the ability to perform automatic cognitive tasks, particularly when measured under pressure to maintain focused attention
- Decision/reaction time/speed

IQ tests in 2015 include:

- Weschler Preschool and Primary Scale of Intelligence, Fourth Edition (WPPSI-IV)
- Weschler Intelligence Scale for Children-IV (WISC-IV), for children of school age
- Weschler Adult Intelligence Scale (WAIS)
- Stanford-Binet Intelligence Scale
- Woodcock-Johnson Tests of Cognitive Ability
- Kaufman Assessment Battery for Children (KABC)
- Cognitive Assessment System (CAS)
- Differentiated Assessment Scales (DAS)

There are also learning issues related to body function:

- Large motor skills
- Fine motor skills
- Proprioception—position and movement sensation
- Exteroception—perception of the outside world
- Interoception—perception of pain, hunger, etc.

Sensory processing disorder is diagnosed when there is sensory sensitivity in visual (sight), auditory (hearing), taste, olfactory (smell), and/or touch. There are several tests used to determine the diagnosis and how to proceed in treatment.

- Sensory Integration and Praxis Test (SIPT)
- DeGangi-Berk Test of Sensory Integration (TSI)
- Test of Sensory Functions in Infants (TSFI)

Standardized questionnaires include:

- Sensory Profile (SP)
- Infant/Toddler Sensory Profile
- Adolescent/Adult Sensory Profile
- Sensory Profile School Companion
- Sensory Processing Measure (SPM)
- Sensory Processing Measure Preschool (SPM-P)

Other tests used include:

- Developmental Test of Visual Perception, Second Edition (DTVP-2)
- Beery-Buktenica Developmental Test of Visual-Motor Integration, 6th Edition (BEERY VMI)
- Miller Function and Participation Scales (M-FUN)
- Bruininks–Oseretsky Test of Motor Proficiency, Second Edition (BOT-2)
- Behavior Rating Inventory of Executive Function (BRIEF)

Gifted or Inductive Reasoning Issues or Both

If you have an L4 in your family, when he or she is young, it may be difficult to determine if you have a gifted child or one who has IRI or both.

Those who are gifted but *don't* have IRI may show the following attributes:

- They will cry as babies.
- When little, they will point at things they want or want to know about them.

- They will ask, "What's that?"
- The number of friends will depend on whether they are an introvert or an extrovert.
- They often have a large vocabulary early and/or will read beyond grade level, and/or they will be outstanding in math and/or science skills.
- They want to understand all possible aspects of something or someone.
- They have an incredible memory.
- They notice all the details.
- They share too many details and bore others or can be socially inappropriate *at times.*
- They have a high focus ability *but can shift topics.*
- They often learn the first time they see or hear something.
- They don't study in school much if at all till later years.
- They love to organize because they hate to waste time.
- They think and process quicker than peers and often adults.
- They think beyond their peers.
- They are often impatient or frustrated that others can't follow them either in speed or how they think.
- They get bored a lot because they learn quickly and retain easily and are ready to move on.
- They are intense.
- They often overwhelm others by their quick thinking or intensity.
- They are often misunderstood by others.
- They don't feel as if they fit in anywhere.
- They can separate Feelings and Thinking.
- They can see the details *and* the big picture.

- They notice patterns that most people miss.
- They don't need rules because they can understand others and their motivations.

They will also develop and use their verbal pragmatic abilities. They are able to:

- Start, maintain, and end conversations appropriately
- Modify language depending upon the audience
- Identify and express feelings, theirs and others'
- Match the moods and emotions of their peers or those in the room
- Monitor and repair verbal interactions
- Monitor and adapt behavior to the situation

They will do much better than those with IRI in their social interactions with others.

Differential Diagnosis

Chapter 2, "Understanding Aspects of Inductive Reasoning Issues," has enough information for you to be able to ask the questions to determine whether the person has social phobia vs. overwhelm, sensory sensitivity vs. overwhelm, resistance to change vs. OCD.

Generally those with IRI have anxiety, and some have social phobia so I always keep IRI in mind when someone has either diagnosis and check for the ability to do empathy.

I've looked at narcissism vs. IRI, and the difference I note is that those who are narcissistic have grandiosity in their thinking. If they don't, then they probably have IRI. (Although I did have one person who had both the grandiosity and IRI.) Those with IRI can have inappropriate expectations for their self or others, but it doesn't usually get expressed as grandiosity.

Some of those diagnosed with ADHD have a stream of consciousness talking to themselves or others without being aware of the impact on others or their relationship with others. When I see that, I check for IRI.

I've worked with some people diagnosed bipolar, and about half of them have had IRI. Sometimes their brain is firing so much they struggle to control their behavior. That is not the same as IRI. I use the worksheets or other pragmatic or social skills testing for them.

Many people who have ADD have been diagnosed with Asperger's and vice versa. I often think they have both Asperger's and ADD or ADHD. ADHD is easy to diagnose because of the hyperactivity. ADD behavior, on the other hand, can be a part of many diagnoses, including ADD, Asperger's, social communication disorder, bipolar, obsessive compulsive disorder (OCD), reactive attachment disorder, oppositional defiant disorder, or anxiety disorder. If you are unsure after reading this book, then checking for pragmatic or social skills can help you determine if this is IRI.

Daniel Amen has defined ADD in six categories which doesn't match the *Diagnostic and Statistical Manual of Mental Disorders* (DSM-5). His classic ADD is the DSM ADHD, inattentive ADD is ADD, overfocused ADD is OCD, temporal lobe ADD is reactive attachment disorder or oppositional defiant, limbic ADD is autism, and ring of fire ADD is bipolar. His book, *Healing ADD*, can be helpful in understanding some of what is going on in the brain for those diagnoses. His questionnaire is good, except for defining issues for those on the autism spectrum or those who have IRI.

Frankly, I don't think we have the best diagnostic tools for IRI, autism, ADD, ADHD, bipolar, and narcissism. I'm looking forward to better tools in the future as we learn more about the brain and how it functions. Hopefully this book will help you identify IRI and give you some information on how to address the issues related to various aspects.

Doing Psychotherapy or Counseling

I've learned as a licensed marriage and family therapist (LMFT) that it is vital to work with clients who have IRI along with a family member. With elementary or younger children, I have a parent stay in the room and watch how I work and talk with the child so the parent can learn to better communicate. I will work with each of them individually at times and with them together at times. With teens or older, I split the session three ways. I take fifteen to twenty minutes with the client with IRI alone, fifteen to twenty minutes with the parent, spouse, or family member(s) alone, and fifteen to twenty minutes with all of them together. That way I can hear what is going on at home and in the world from the perspective of the person with IRI who often has a very different worldview. With the family member(s), I can get a view of how the person with IRI is impacting others in the world and what I may need to teach the person with IRI about relationships and how to interact. Working with them all together allows me to work on their relationship, their understanding of each other, and their expectations.

Each party often struggles to understand things that the other does and needs some explanation. If I do this apart, it allows me to say things without being careful about the impact on each other. I can get family history without boring the person with IRI who may not understand or care about it. Splitting the session keeps attention going in the person who has IRI who often loses attention, focus, or patience after about fifteen to twenty minutes.

If you don't work this way and you want to try it, I suggest letting your client know that for the next X amount of time you will work this way. Then you will evaluate together what is needed and decide whether to continue splitting the session or change it. Having a regular three- or four-month review can be helpful. Sometimes I work by phone with some introvert clients on the spectrum for two out of four sessions a month. It depends on how they handle talking on the phone. I need to be able to see them often enough to actually see their reactions. I also want to recognize and adapt to how much being around people increases their anxiety. Phone time can lower their anxiety enough for them to hear better what I have to say, at least in the beginning. The goal over time is that we work live weekly as anxiety is reduced and social skill training can increase. Sometimes talking on the phone does not work at all, so I don't commit to more than one session on the phone at a time. That way we can determine if that will actually be helpful or not.

Working on social skills training in small groups of four to six depending on the number of introverts is very helpful. It may need to go on for a long time depending on their Level of Impact. This can be more affordable than individual therapy for that long, and they can learn from each other. It can allow for some consistency while still working on changing behavior.

I recognize the need for extroverts to verbally process. I don't expect them to understand or translate to other situations any better than the introverts just because they are talking about it. You have to figure out their level of understanding and the level at which you need to work with them.

I find that asking yes-or-no questions to be the most helpful in the beginning. I have also found that I have to ask very specific questions if they are not yes-and-no ones. I have learned to think about what information I want and then form a question that will focus exactly on that information. This takes practice. So I'm often correcting myself along the way. If the client is a Level 4, I can also use my corrections to indicate how others may form their questions and how the person with IRI can then ask for clarification. And I work at telling the person the connections between similar situations.

Asking a why question will often make it impossible for clients with IRI to figure out what information you are actually seeking. Asking who, what, when, where, and how questions will get the information you are seeking. Teaching them to identify those types of questions will help them know how to respond more appropriately.

Teaching them to ask others to clarify a why question helps others formulate more helpful questions.

I have found when asking if those with IRI are feeling anxious that they often don't know how to label what they feel. I have written what stress, worry, fear, anxiety, and panic are like so they can determine what they are actually feeling. I've also defined levels of mad, sad, scared, and glad. Defining opposites can be a very helpful way to understand and identify emotions—happy vs. sad, anxious vs. calm, etc. Having feeling scales can be very helpful in defining the feeling at a low, medium, or high level and to learn what behavior is appropriate for each level.

Chapter 5 | Working with Those Who Have Inductive Reasoning Issues

Basic Guidelines for Us to Help Them

Here are some basic guidelines that can be helpful in general when you are interacting with those with IRI.

1. Give them more processing time and understand that they are working really hard.
2. Know that in groups they may shut down at some point because their system has reached overload. This will be more obvious in children. They may express frustration/anger, but we often interpret the reason incorrectly. Students or children are not necessarily being oppositional. They are trying to protect themselves from being overwhelmed. They may get up and leave without saying anything. Older children or people will look wide-eyed at us, but we get the sense they aren't really there, or they look away and don't have any eye contact.
3. Stop when you see they are shutting down or overwhelmed. Do something different. But come back later to unfinished issues or discussion.
4. Learn to be clear in your communication so your question asks for the exact information you are seeking.
5. Avoid idioms, colloquialisms, sayings.
6. Avoid why questions; instead use who, what, when, where, how.

7. Learn ways to manage your frustration until you can fully understand and work with them at their level, accept them at that level, and still have ways to cope with your frustration after that.
8. Change your interpretations of their behavior so that you don't feel hurt, frustrated, neglected, angry, etc.

This takes work on our part, but those with IRI are always working very hard in their relationships. It will be to everyone's benefit if we can give them some extra understanding and space. And get support for yourself if you are a parent or partner of someone who has IRI. It can be very taxing and frustrating and in the beginning painful and grief filled. (See the Grief section in "Resources.")

Scaling Anything

One of the difficulties that some IRI folks have is applying a scale to things. I just accept whatever level they need to use. Some want to over-define, like 6.28 on a scale of one to ten. Or they struggle to identify what level on a one-to-ten scale. It can take them longer to figure out a level than to identify what they are feeling or experiencing. For those folks, I learned to use a zero-to-four point system so they could figure out things faster.

Zero = none, never, nothing

One = some or sometimes

Two = medium, half or half of the time

Three = a lot or most of the time

Four = always or all the time

They don't need more things to figure out, and this gives most of us enough information to be useful. Those who are more literal may need to set up their own scale, and it's good to ask them if they need that. These folks may be able to use a hundred-point system the best.

Working on Aspects

I always work on sensory sensitivities first. They can cause negative behaviors as the person with IRI tries to protect themselves from additional overwhelm. It also interferes with their ability to focus on other things. Generally, when you can reduce the sensitivity some of the negative behaviors will subside.

Start working with only one aspect at a time per session. I start working on the behaviors that impact them negatively out in the world. I often work on one aspect towards others and then one aspect in being more aware of themselves. As they gain mastery you add another aspect.

It's important to make clear, concrete agreements about how the person with IRI will work on an aspect and how family members or teachers will help them. Set regular times to review how things are progressing with each party involved. I may start with monthly reviews and then lengthen the time as progress is made. If the person with IRI gets stuck it's important to work on that issue until there is understanding or the conflict is resolved.

Working with Children Who Have Inductive Reasoning Issues

Sometimes those with IRI struggle with the grief process but aren't aware of it. A parent can see the change in behavior, but children with IRI may not be aware of their behavior. If someone points out their behavior to them, they may not know why they are acting the way they are acting. They may need to be educated on what different feelings feel like in their body, the different levels of feelings, the names for feelings, and how to express them appropriately.

Because they struggle to make meaning, they often don't interpret having IRI as being personally defective. We all have different things that are easy for us and hard for us, with most things somewhere in-between. Unless someone talks with them about IRI in a way that defines them as being "sick" or "defective," they probably won't go there in their thinking. So, be careful what you say to them or in front of them. Help them understand what they need to learn without making it define who they are. None of our behavior defines who we are. We all have the option of changing behavior, feelings, viewpoints, etc. And all of us are wired differently. See chapter 5 for other resources. If there are limited resources in your area and you want to work with a psychotherapist, ask them to read this book and then work with you to learn how to work with the person with IRI.

Working with Teens Who Have Inductive Reasoning Issues

When teens with IRI experience puberty, they often scramble more that teens who can do inductive reasoning. You will need to do more crisis management depending on how much of a Feeler they are. It's a time to help them cope more than a time to direct their learning. Use immediate experiences at school and with peers to help them learn or reinforce past learning about what will help them in that social situation. As with all teens, this may be a time parents need to use other professionals, like a psychotherapist, to help their child learn instead of doing most of the teaching themselves. Some teens have no problem with working with their parents; others are extremely reactive. School counselors have limited time to offer. There are some socials skills groups offered in larger communities. There are an increasing number of psychotherapists who understand IRI. It is generally well worth the money to have your teen see one.

Working with Adults Who Have Inductive Reasoning Issues

I work with individuals by having them go through this book and fill out the worksheets. I try to pay attention to not only what they tell me but also what I experience immediately in the session. If an aspect occurs, I point it out to them and explore what they were thinking when they said or did that aspect. I talk with them about how it impacted me or how it would impact most people. I share how others would think about it and why. I talk with them about whether they would like to change that response from others and, if so, what they could do differently. If at all possible, I try to get a family member or good friend in periodically so I can hear how the person with IRI has been doing out in the world from the other's perspective. On occasion a boss can willing to be helpful. I think it is more difficult to help adults with IRI when you do not have others outside of the therapy room to give feedback and information because different social situations can raise different aspects.

Working with Parents of Those Who Have Inductive Reasoning Issues

I find it takes about a year of working with parents who can do inductive reasoning to really understand IRI and its impact. Once they understand, they begin to work much better with their child. It's like learning a new language and culture—literally—for both parent and child. Parents have to let go of their dreams and expectations for their child or children with IRI and really meet them where they are developmentally—both in their thinking and in their feeling. That often does not match with their chronological age. These children are generally from one to four years behind socially if they are L3 or L4. And sometimes they are way ahead in their thinking in certain respects. So it's very different and similar to raising a gifted child.

It can be very difficult for parents to learn their child has IRI. They will grieve about each aspect their child has, and it's important to give them support to say whatever they need to say away from their child with IRI. Parents may feel devastated that they can't relate well, blame themselves, blame their partner, or feel frustrated that their child makes social mistakes. They may struggle to understand what they can really expect from their child developmentally. They will grieve and may feel depressed at times. They often feel as if they are on call all the time. One or both parents may have to give up their career choices to have the time or flexibility to parent their child.

It's important that parents get the support they need to raise a child who has IRI. Hopefully this book has been helpful and the resources listed will be helpful. See a therapist that knows about IRI or social communication disorder. Psychotherapists need to educate themselves if they don't know about IRI to work well with a client who has IRI. If parents don't find a psychotherapist who understands IRI, they will be educating their therapist instead of getting the help they need. If there are limited resources in your area, ask the psychotherapist to read this book and then work with you to learn. Parents should find a support group, an ongoing one if they can, because raising a child with IRI is difficult. Parents need to find times and ways to give themselves a break from parenting and take time for themselves. They need to process their feelings and shift their thinking. They need to change their negative thinking if it stays for very long.

It's important that parents spend time keeping the marriage or partnership going well or improving. Taking small vacations away from parenting can be really rejuvenating. The more stability parents can offer their child through a good partner relationship where they are working together to raise this child, the more their child with IRI will be able to deal with the everyday anxieties. The child won't have to manage the additional stressors related to unexpected routines or unexpected parent behavior due to ongoing conflict or divorce.

It can be helpful to have parents meet as a group of four to six over time and read through this book. They can brainstorm ways to work on an aspect. It can be helpful to have a professional that facilitates it who understands IRI. The professional can keep the group on topic, make sure everyone gets a chance to share personal experiences and ideas, and direct how to share ideas in non-judgmental ways. If you don't have a professional that can do this, it may work for group members to trade off that role or at least two of the members trade off that role. Then if the leader wants to share they can turn the group over to the other leader while they share. If a parent has IRI and his or her child has IRI, I don't recommend the parent participate in a group because he or she takes longer to process and often needs explanation. This will keep the group from being as open or able to share.

Working with Partners of Those Who Have Inductive Reasoning Issues

It can be difficult learning a partner has IRI. There will be grief in the recognition that one doesn't have the partner they thought they had. The partner without IRI has to change their expectations of their partner with IRI and of the relationship. But it might also be greatly relieving to finally understand the behavior of the partner with IRI and not take it personally when he or she is unable to be empathic. There's often a history of pain in the relationship that needs to be resolved. Working individually with the partner who does not have IRI some of the time is helpful. A support group for partners can also be helpful.

Working with Couples or Partners Together

All couples have to work at communicating well and understanding one another for the relationship to work well and grow. Those who don't have IRI process information much faster than those with IRI so I don't meet as often with them. I find that I alternate sessions. I'll have one session with the couple to find out the conflicts and decide what we will work on together. Then I meet individually with the person with IRI. That way I can help them sort their feelings, thoughts and needs. I can also explain more about what the partner was saying or needing and what most partners expect. Then I'll have a session with the partner who does not have IRI to help them understand what the person with IRI was thinking and feeling and needing and perhaps work on resolving old hurts. Then I'll meet again with the person with IRI in order to clarify anything or find out what they need to talk about in the next couple session. I may also help them resolve past hurts. Then I'll meet with the couple again to clarify if anything has not been resolved and finish resolving it. I alternate taking issues from each person to address in the couples session. That way there is a sense of equal needs, equal valuing, and equal responsibility. I spend the extra session with the person with IRI in recognition of his or her need for more time to process.

Working with Families with One Who Has Inductive Reasoning Issues

I recommend that families work with a psychotherapist in order to keep conversation focused, keep to only one aspect at a time, and get help with family patterns as well as resolving conflict. I start by meeting with all of the teens or adults in the family without the family member who has IRI. I explain IRI to all of them and answer any questions they have about IRI. Then I work with the individual with IRI and help them to understand their aspects and answer their questions. If it's a child, I work with at least one parent present. I shared how I split the time with teens who have IRI. Then I work with various family members in different combinations over time depending on the age, the aspects and the level of conflicts. Sometimes I work individually, sometimes with two at a time. I rarely work with more than two family members at a time because that is often overwhelming for the person with IRI. Often when a sibling with IRI gets better, other siblings will want to retaliate for what they have endured so far. It's best to work with them individually without their sibling that has IRI to resolve their grief and pain.

Working with Teachers of Students with Inductive Reasoning Issues

Teachers have a very difficult job today. They have a very broad range of abilities in the students in their class, and they have to try to teach to all the levels. They have limited help and resources, especially with children who have behavior or learning issues. There are often too many children in a class to teach well. The majority of teachers really want to do well at their job, and they want their students to learn. I find that if I come from a compassionate place in interacting with teachers I get a very good response from them. They often are not trained about IRI, although that is beginning to change, especially among the special education staff. I worked in the school system for a couple of years, and

I have a lot of respect for school staff who are working hard and often without enough resources or staff to help.

I've written one-to-two-page explanations of many aspects of IRI. They are available on my website at www.Counsel-Heal.com. I recommend sending them attached to an email or letter. Explain how you see that aspect displayed in the child's behavior and any ideas that you found worked well in working with the child. Parents or psychotherapists can do this for students. Most teachers have given a very positive response and have either thanked me or told me how they caught themselves and changed how they said something. Or they explained things like idioms to the student. I've sent letters to teachers, principals, school counselors, and the special education staff.

You will need a release from a parent or the student if he or she is thirteen or older. You may want to have students and parents sign an agreement about how much you will share via email, texts or letters. You may want to call or send a letter instead of email if you include the diagnosis in order to meet HIPAA standards. You will have to decide the confidentiality and security issues that email creates. You can send letters by secure email, but some staff are less likely to open them.

I recommend sending the school staff the first letter explaining you will be sending short articles most weeks to help them understand and work with the student. Ask staff to contact you if they have any questions. I recommend not sending out anything the first or last three weeks of school. It is just too busy for the staff to be able to read it. Don't send out articles on the last or first week of quarters or trimesters or before and after major breaks during the year. If you have all-year schooling, avoid the one to two weeks before and after each break. School staff are usually organizing themselves, and they won't have time to read your messages. Often they are required to read correspondence from parents, but timing can effect what they retain in their memory from the information. You can often get about twenty sent in a school year.

Working with Children of Those Who Have Inductive Reasoning Issues

Children of those who have IRI need to be educated on IRI and how it affects their parent. Otherwise they will misunderstand their parent's behavior and assume they are the problem or their parent doesn't care about them.

For those children of parents who have IRI, it can heal the relationship to know that the lack of empathy, of caring behavior, of initiating contact, or the demands to be just like their parent stem from the parent's inability to do inductive reasoning. This was a personal one for me. I tried to work on the relationship with my father for many years. I thought he chose to not understand or change his behavior. I found that I could not understand his choices, motivations, or behavior, and I gave up at one point. Understanding that his brain couldn't understand a lot of what I was saying or that he didn't know how to respond was really helpful. And learning how to talk with him was healing for us both.

Final Comments

Working with those who have IRI is different from most therapy because they have to learn appropriate social skills directly and specifically in order to get along in the world. If they had good parents, but the parents didn't know there were inductive reasoning issues, they probably didn't give their children with IRI direct verbal instructions to help them. So you have to teach them. Clients have to consciously change unhelpful rules they created in order to function better in their family or make sense of the world. And these rules may not be obvious to you or to them.

You will have to figure out the right question to ask in order to find some issues or understand the thinking of those with IRI. Working with those who have IRI is a slower and longer process than with most clients. You will have to be patient for them to answer a question and not interrupt their thinking with more input or questions. You will need to continue to learn how to ask very specific questions and not use common language, idioms or colloquialisms. You will have to catch when you do and reword comments or questions. Consulting with someone who can do this well or being a part of an IRI consultation group can be very helpful.

Final Overview

1. We are all unique, and we all understand things a little differently. Be compassionate with one another.
2. Ask a specific question to get the specific information you want.
3. Don't assume the other person is lying until you understand what he or she was thinking.
4. If you don't understand something, ask a friend or the person in charge for the information you need. Don't wait, but do learn to choose socially appropriate times to ask, or make notes to remember and ask later.
5. If you thought you understood something and you didn't, apologize. Then say what you thought the other person wanted or what he or she meant, and ask if you were correct or not. Ask for more information. Then again share what you understand. Keep asking and sharing until the other person tells you that you understand correctly.
6. Don't demand too many new things. New things are usually a drain for those with IRI. Extroverts will handle new things a little better than introverts, but new things are often not as fun or exciting as they are for those who can do inductive reasoning.
7. Those with sensory sensitivity issues can't help it, so don't be upset with them. Be caring and help them cope.
8. Don't demand too much of those with IRI. They are working really hard all the time with any social interaction.
9. Get support, education, and therapies when you need them.

Resources

Getting Help

We are taught as psychotherapists that how you were raised causes you to behave the way you do. If your parents were good-enough parents, you became a pretty functional adult, able to manage basic needs like maintaining food, clothing, shelter, a job, and relationships that last. If they weren't good enough, you have behavior issues and thinking that gets you in trouble or causes you to struggle with being able to get or keep a job, meet your basic needs, and have relationships that last. Either way, you generally have relationships that look like those of your parents or like your relationship with one parent. If you had good-enough parents, you will have pretty healthy interactions that make you generally feel pretty good. If you had unhealthy parents, you will have relationships where you are sad or angry or afraid most of the time.

Trauma occurs when you are treated in a way that intentionally hurts you emotionally, physically, or sexually or when you see others treated in a way that intentionally hurts them emotionally, physically or sexually. Sometimes people don't mean to be hurtful, but they can't control their own behavior and continue to be hurtful. Some people do it on purpose. Trauma and shock can occur with sudden shocking experiences, like watching a car accident where someone is killed or a hurricane that destroys things around you. If you have someone you can talk to about what happened, who can help you make sense of things you have questions about, you can talk to about how you feel, and can recognize your experience and feelings, then you can resolve the trauma so that it doesn't bother you anymore. You need to take as much time as it takes for you to resolve the issue.

If you don't have someone listen to your thoughts, answer questions, and support you in various feelings, making sense of what happened and letting go of the trauma in the memories, then you will continue to hold on to the memories and relive or repeat them in various ways until you can get them resolved. Your behavior will form around managing or avoiding the memories or the feelings or the thoughts that trouble you that aren't resolved. And yet part of you will still want to resolve it. So, people will often marry someone like the parent they have the most issues with that are unresolved because it forces people to face their issues. The more unresolved trauma or shock one experiences, the greater the amount and/or intensity of abnormal behavior. Because behavior is learned from one generation to another, the trauma can be recent or in generations past. Both can affect behavior.

Our job as psychotherapists is to help those who want to change. We are trained to help you identify and resolve old issues and help you change your thinking and behavior so you will be happier and function better and your relationships will be happier and healthier.

There are many modalities or ways of doing therapy. We may teach you new behavior that is more helpful. We may teach you new ways of thinking that help you change your feelings about yourself or others. We may give you things to practice or do that change your interactions with others. We may teach you to be in touch with all your feelings and how to deal with and express all of them appropriately. We may look at what the triggers are that cause the feelings and behavior to occur that aren't helpful to you or to your relationships. We can help you to change the trigger or the reaction to the trigger. Following in this resources section, I've included types of therapy and how they can help and an outline on the grief process.

Types of Therapists and Doctors

Throughout the book, I have used the term psychotherapist, which stands for marriage and family therapist, mental health counselor, or social worker, all of which have specific training in counseling various issues. Most psychotherapists have learned how to help people with depression, anxiety, thought patterns, and grief. The majority have been taught to some degree in how to diagnose using the *Diagnostic and Statistical Manual of Mental Disorders,* or DSM-5, which is now in its fifth edition. Each educational institute granting a degree in a therapy will define its degree a little differently, and each state will have different requirements for certification or licensure.

As of 2015, I've not heard of any counseling training program that teaches psychotherapists to assess or teach social skills. Most psychotherapists are learning on their own because they have a family member that has IRI or they are interested in that population. Resources have developed out of counseling and speech therapy to help with emotions and with social thinking.

Below is more information that can help you choose someone to help you that best fits you and your needs.

Marriage and Family Therapist

A licensed marriage and family therapist, or LMFT, has a bachelor's or master's degree in some form of counseling. LMFTs train an additional two thousand hours to learn about family dynamics (patterns of behaviors and roles within the family), how dynamics will appear in therapy, and how to help families change the dynamics or behaviors. Families organize around those with IRI or any major diagnosis or disability because the person needs extra help. This can create dynamics that aren't helpful for the individual or family. LMFTs can help with both the issues and the family dynamics. They are almost always masters' level therapists.

Mental Health Counselor

A licensed mental health counselor, or LMHC, has a bachelor's degree and sometimes a master's degree in something related to counseling. There is a great variety of training programs for those who get this certification or license depending on the state they practice in. Be sure to ask what their training is in and how it can help you. Check their credentials, knowledge of social communication disorder and autism spectrum issues, and history of working with them.

Psychiatrist

Psychiatrists are good at evaluations and medications but rarely know much about how to help create change through changes in thinking or behavior. If they do therapy, it's usually Freudian in nature, which is very non-directive. Working with IRI requires a lot of education and direction. If you need medication, I recommend finding a psychiatrist who understands aspects of autism. DAN! doctors may be able to help. See below.

Psychologist

Psychologists often do testing and evaluations and have areas of specialty where they do therapy of some kind. Some just do evaluations and testing. They have training in medications but not to the level of being able to prescribe. There are many training programs with various specialties, so you have to find out if they know anything about working with Autistic populations or social communication disorder and their history of working with them.

Social Worker

A licensed social worker, or LSW, helps those who need additional services with the state or city and coordinates care in a variety of settings. Some train in modalities for counseling and become counselors. Again, check their credentials, knowledge of social communication disorder and autism spectrum issues, and history of working with them.

Coach

Coaches have become popular now that there is a lot of online information and training. Many of them don't have training in therapy or much training at all, so be sure to check out their credentials and training before using them. They, as a group, don't have any organization that oversees them for appropriate treatments, confidentiality, or behavior. All the others listed in this section do. Find out if the coach knows anything about working with Autistic populations or social communication disorder and his or her history of working with them.

Christian, Pastoral, or Existential Therapist

These people deal with our beliefs about and relationship with God or a higher power/organizing force. These folks may have a whole variety of credentials, including being a pastor or therapist, or no credentials. They often don't have any organization that oversees them for appropriate treatments, confidentiality, or behavior. Many therapists address these issues but don't call themselves a Christian, pastoral, or existential therapist. Again, check their credentials, knowledge of social communication disorder and autism spectrum issues, and history of working with them.

Speech Therapist

This specialist often works with children in the school settings or learning centers on speech or social skills. They have developed most of the tools that we are using now for social communication disorder.

Occupational Therapist

An occupational therapist, or OT, works with fine motor skills, like holding a pencil, which is often an issue for those on the autism spectrum, Asperger's, or social communication disorders.

Physical Therapist

A physical therapist, or PT, works with the larger muscle groups to help children be better connected to their body, move well, or recover from car or other accidents.

Vision Therapist

This person is trained in various techniques that train your eyes to work together. A vision therapist works closely with an optometrist or ophthalmologist who will do the ongoing testing to see what exercises you need to correct your vision. You can find information and optometrists and ophthalmologists trained to evaluate vision issues at www.HomeVisionTherapy.com/doctors_state_index.htm.

Naturopath

Naturopaths have a variety of training and interests. They focus on how to get your body healthy. They may work with diet, tinctures, homeopathic substances, or supplements to help you become healthier. Many work with you to improve digestion, which is key to having a healthy body. Check with them for their area of expertise.

Medical Doctors

Medical doctors (MDs), or physicians, are trained in disease and surgery and usually have a specialty in some area. They are trained and can prescribe medications for both physical and mental issues. They often don't have any training in nutrition or supplements or how to help your body become healthier. They generally just relieve discomfort with medication and don't address the underlying issue that created it.

Defeat Autism Now! Doctor

DAN! doctors follow the DAN! protocol, which involves unconventional treatment methods, like Methyl B-12 injections, nutritional supplements, chelation, intravenous immunoglobulin (IVIG) treatment, and implementation of the gluten-free dairy-free (GFDF) diet. Many parents have claimed tremendous success in treating their children with autism using DAN! Doctors. You can find a partial list at: www.healing-arts.org/children/amyholmes.htm#danlist.

Neurologist

This specialist has specific training in the brain and what affects brain function. He or she will look for disease, damage, or sleep apnea and may work with drugs and supplements to improve function.

Nutritionist

This individual is trained specifically in nutrition, how the body digests food, and the nutrients that it needs to be healthy. They can be a helpful resource to use, especially if you have poor eating habits. They often know a lot about supplements and how they affect your body as well. Your insurance may cover a nutritionist but not a naturopath.

Chiropractor

Chiropractors focus on helping your body become healthier by using manual manipulation and massage to adjust the spine to relieve tension and pain. This can be a great temporary relief but often does not address the underlying issue. You may have one leg longer than the other, or emotional or relational issues may be creating the tension that is causing your back to go out of alignment.

Types of Therapy and What They Address

There are many types of therapy. You can go to Wikipedia and search for psychotherapies, and you will get a huge list. Below is a brief summary of some types of therapy that I've found to be the most helpful to those with IRI. I've included mind-and-body modalities that Wikipedia will not carry or will disparage because of lack of knowledge or experience with them.

I think the most important thing to start with in therapy is coping skills so that people survive well in their daily life while they make the changes they want to make.

Coping Skills

Clients need to plan for how to manage what they struggle with on a daily basis. They need to learn how to solve personal and relationship problems and seek to master, minimize, or tolerate stress, conflict, and emotions.

Emotional Coping

It's important to learn to identify feelings and to learn to manage and express them appropriately. Learning about the grief process and getting help to work through it fully can be one of the most helpful things you can do for your health and well-being, whether you have IRI or not.

Understanding Shock and Trauma

It's really important to understand the difference between trauma and shock so that working with the trauma doesn't increase the shock. The treatments for each are very different. Not many people are trained in identifying shock and working with it to release it from the body system. Trauma work done while people are in shock will increase the shock and keep one from resolving the trauma.

Understanding Trauma. Trauma occurs when we have an experience where the result is an overwhelming amount of stress that exceeds one's ability to cope or keeps one from integrating the emotions involved with that experience. We have to make meaning (come to understand what happened and why) that allows us to resolve the feelings. We need to get support in having our feelings and in expressing our feelings in appropriate ways to move on from the trauma. Otherwise, in the future we avoid what caused the trauma or things similar to what caused the trauma and limit our life. And we have to manage the unresolved emotions that sit in our body and cause us tension.

Understanding Shock. This is a very primitive body response to danger, and there are two levels. The first is when we are startled and freeze to identify the danger. (Most people have experienced this when a door slams unexpectedly.) Then our body goes into fight or flight, which is sympathetic shock. We get ready to fight what is threatening us or to flee from it. It is difficult to think when you are scanning constantly for danger. I believe those with ADHD and bipolar have this going all the time and can't turn it off.

If we can't fight or flee, then our body goes into para-sympathetic shock, slows down, and plays dead. We do not want to be noticed so that we can avoid being attacked.

If your body is in shock and you try to do the cathartic work of expressing your feelings, especially forcefully, your body may become more tense rather than relieved. If that occurs, you need to look for body cues for shock. Shock needs very quiet, gentle talk and expression of feelings with perhaps a gentle touch on a knee or hand or upper back in order for the body to come out of the fight-or-flight response or the play-dead response. It's best to work with a psychotherapist that understands shock in order to relieve it. There are not a lot of them.

Get Consultation

It can be difficult to identify and learn how to treat those with IRI. I do consultation for psychotherapists or teachers who are needing help to determine if someone has IRI and how to work with those with IRI. I also do consultation on how to identify and treat shock. See my website, www.Counsel-Heal.com, for more information.

Thinking Modalities in Psychotherapy That Can Help with IRI

- *Cognitive Behavioral Therapy* (CBT) deals with how you are thinking about things and how you can change your thinking and your emotional responses to things. You can change negative thinking, your interpretation of what occurred, and your emotional response to things you have experienced.
- *Dialectical Behavior Therapy* (DBT) combines standard CBT and reality-testing with concepts of distress tolerance, acceptance, and mindful awareness (being in the moment and not lost in thoughts or feelings).
- *Social Skills Training* helps people learn how to interact and communicate in socially acceptable ways. One learns about social rules and how relationships are created, communicated, and changed in verbal and nonverbal ways. All those with IRI need this training.

Mind and Body Modalities in Psychotherapy That Can Help with IRI

The general medical profession often doesn't recognize the helpfulness of these modalities. Most of them are still gathering research that validates their use. I have used all of them with great results, so I include them here. You can visit my website, www.Counsel-Heal.com, for more explanation and links to their websites.

- *Developmental Kinesiology* evaluates the sixteen reflexes that are developed in utero through the first year of life. Reflexes need to be developed fully, integrated fully, and all but five of them need to be turned off until our body needs them. The fight-or-flight response is one of them that gets stuck on, and this modality can help you manage or even turn off this response.
- *Brain Gym/Educational Kinesiology* uses a combination of body and eye movement, affirmations, tapping or sweeping meridians, resonation, and working with neurovascular points to allow the brain and body to reorganize around a new way of thinking or feeling about a past experience. It is a way to resolve shock and trauma.
- *Eye Movement Desensitization and Reprocessing* (EMDR) allows people to resolve trauma through focusing on the issue while moving their eyes back and forth, experiencing tapping alternating on their hands or knees or hearing a tapping sound alternating in their ears.
- *Energy Psychology/Thought Field Therapy/Emotional Freedom Technique* sets goals for change, then clears objections to change, and creates change by tapping on points located on the meridian systems of the body or working with the chakras or biofield. This tends to shift things quickly, so you have to be ready for that.
- *Energy Medicine* works with a variety of energy systems in the body to create health and well-being and clear trauma, physical pain, and illness.
- *Pre- and Pari-natal Shock and Trauma.* All our reflexes develop in utero through the first year of life. They need to be developed, integrated and most of them turned off. You can work to clear

the shock and then deal with the trauma using any method above.

- *Touch for Health* is a method to balance the body towards health by tapping/rubbing or holding neurovascular points to balance the body system.

Grief Information

Grief is usually thought of as sadness due to a loss. Elisabeth Kubler-Ross expanded that into stages of grief, but she dealt with the dying. Bertha Simos wrote an excellent book on grief for those who are living, *A Time to Grieve: Loss as Life Experience.* It was written for professionals and is no longer in print but still can be found used or sometimes even new. The major difference in grieving by the dying and the living is that those who are dying do bargaining and those who are living do searching behavior. Understanding searching behavior can be very helpful and relieving to those who are experiencing it.

Often in families there is one or more feelings that aren't OK to express. Sometimes family members learned to express feelings in ways that are damaging to relationships or to themselves. Most of us haven't learned how to grieve fully or are in the process of learning it. Taking time to learn and do your grief work will help you be physically and mentally healthier. You will more often be able to respond the way you want to respond instead of reacting. A psychotherapist can take clients only as far as he or she has come.

Grief generally comes with recognizing there is IRI. Parents may search for the cause of IRI, search for a cure for IRI, continue searching for resources to help IRI, and search for positive signs and behaviors from their child with IRI. Parents don't expect to have a child with IRI and need to grieve the lost dreams about their child and family. It's important to identify those things that have been lost (hopes, dreams, expectations, etc.) or have been given up (going some places, taking a vacation as a family, career choices, etc.) in dealing with IRI. There will be a variety of things, and different things will surface in awareness at different times and with different developmental stages.

Sometimes those with IRI are struggling with the grief process, but they aren't aware of it. Parents or partners may see the behavior. Those with IRI need help to identify feelings, the intensity of their feelings, and how they experience them in their body. They need coaching on how to express their feelings appropriately or manage them in social situations.

People will spend varying amounts of time in each part of the grief process. There is no set order within Phase 2 or within Phase 3. You may revisit parts that you thought you had completed. I encourage you to set aside time each night, even if it's ten to fifteen minutes, to process the day. Then things won't collect and weigh you down or make you sick.

The first page is an outline of most of the information from *A Time to Grieve: Loss as Life Experience* by Bertha Simos. The pages that follow have some explanations to help you understand the different parts of the grieving process listed on the first page.

Phases of Grief Outline

Phase 1: Shock, alarm, denial, and bargaining

Phase 2: Acute grief consisting of:

- Continuing, intermittent, and lessening denial
- Physical and psychological pain and distress
- Ambivalence with contradictory pulls, emotions and impulses
- Searching behavior and attempts at retrieval
    - Preoccupation with thoughts of the loss
    - A compulsion to speak of the loss
    - A compulsion to retrieve that which was lost

    - A sense of waiting for something to happen
    - Aimless wandering and restlessness
    - A feeling of being lost, of not knowing what to do
    - A feeling of disorganization
    - A sense that time isn't moving forward normally, feeling stuck in the past
    - A feeling that life can never be worthwhile again
    - Confusion and feelings that things are not real
    - Fear that all the above indicate mental illness
- Crying, anger, guilt, shame
- Identifying with traits, values, symptoms, tastes, or other characteristics of the lost one
- Regression or return to behaviors and feelings of an earlier age, or connected with a previous loss or reactions towards that loss
- Helplessness and depression
- Hopelessness and hope
- Relief and restoration of meaning
- Restitution
- Depletion
- Decrease in pain and increasing capacity to cope over time
- A compulsion to find meaning in the loss
- Beginning thoughts of a new life without the lost person/object

Phase 3: Integration of the loss and grief

- If the outcome is favorable:
    - Acceptance of the reality of the loss and return to physical and psychological well-being
    - Diminished frequency and intensity of crying

    - Restored self-esteem
    - Focus on the present and future
    - Ability to enjoy life again
    - Pleasure at awareness of growth from the experience
    - Reorganization of a new identity with restitution for the loss
    - Loss remembered with poignancy and caring instead of pain
- If the outcome is unfavorable:
    - Acceptance of the reality of the loss with lingering sense of depression and physical aches and pains
    - Diminished sense of self-esteem
    - Reorganization of a new identity with constriction of personality and involvement
    - Vulnerability to other separations and losses

Grief is intense emotional suffering caused by loss, disaster, misfortune; it is acute sorrow, deep sadness with episodic pangs (feelings of severe anxiety and/or psychological pain).

Categories of loss include:

1. significant person or who you thought the person was
2. part of the self
3. external objects
4. developmental loss

Phases of Grief Explained

Phase 1: Shock, Alarm, Denial, and Bargaining

Shock and Alarm

If loss comes without warning, there is shock. There's a sense of things not being real, and we stop feeling. The reaction to shock is alarm and anxiety about the change to come. The way we cope initially is with denial.

Denial

After shock and alarm, we reach denial. This is a shutting out of awareness that would be too disturbing to know. Forms of denial include:

- Disbelief in recognizing the loss
    - Denial of the reality of the loss; it can be to the extent of shutting out all awareness of surroundings or of the issue
    - Uncertainty about the finality of the loss, which increases denial
    - Resistance to dependency, especially seen in teens and adults
    - Refusing to believe those we trust may have let us down
- Cognitive recognition. This can occur without the accompanying feelings or with an isolation of the feelings. There can be a denial of the importance of the lost object/person through contempt, devaluation, or depreciation.
- Focus on what is left that is not lost without the feelings of loss
- Phantom limb experience—feeling sensations from the lost part of the body

Denial can take the form of hectic searching for a replacement of the lost object/person, or it may take the form of fantasies about the lost object/person.

Denial is best dealt with by the supportive presence of an understanding person. Given enough time and the opportunity to talk, the normally grieving person will begin to take in the loss. Talking needs to be accompanied by the expression of feelings, not just talking about the feelings.

Denial allows us to take in the loss at a rate that we can process.

Bargaining

This is the attempt to postpone the inevitable. It is a way to decrease anxiety by resting our case with a higher power. You may or may not do bargaining unless an impending death is the loss.

Phase 2: Acute Grief

This next phase consists of the following reactions:

Continuing, Intermittent (On and Off), and Lessening Denial

Physical and Psychological Pain and Distress

The physical reaction can include the inability to sleep or having psychological reactions. Weight loss or gain, anorexia, diarrhea, constipation, and respiratory ailments are all common. Physical distress arouses more anxiety, which can lead the bereaved to seek medical help. If the doctor doesn't find anything, it can be dealt with as grief. Loss can precipitate physical diseases when the feelings are not released and the tension is held over a long period of time.

Ambivalence

Ambivalence is when you have conflicting impulses or feelings and pulls to do different or opposite things. Our beliefs about various feelings or criticism about those feelings will add feelings about the feelings to the process. This can hinder progress through the grief process and resolution of the grief.

Searching and Attempts at Retrieval

Searching behavior can include:

- Preoccupation with thoughts and images of lost object/person
- A compulsion to speak of the loss
- A compulsion to retrieve that which was lost
- A sense of waiting for something to happen
- Aimless wandering and restlessness
- A sense that time isn't moving forward normally
- Feeling stuck in the past
- A feeling of being lost, of not knowing what to do
- A feeling of disorganization or actual disorganization
- Inability to initiate any activity
- Effort to accomplish previously routine tasks
- Lack of zest or interest in daily living activities
- A feeling of going through the motions of living
- A feeling that life can never be worthwhile again
- Confusion and feelings that things are not real
- Fear that all of the above indicate mental illness

Crying, Anger, Guilt, Shame

Crying

Crying and yearning are ways to reconnect with others. Some crying can be done alone, but not all. Reconnection will occur when the listener understands and the bereaved feels safe in their vulnerability to share their tears.

Anger

Anger can be directed inward or outward. Anger directed outward can include:

- Anger at those believed to be responsible for the loss—doctor, agency, police, God, relatives
- Anger at a scapegoat, a lashing out in place of feeling guilt or helplessness
- Anger directed inward can include:
- Depression
- Nightmares
- Psychosomatic disorders
- Organic disorders
- Ruminations about a dreadful past
- Suicide or suicidal thoughts

Anger can be outbursts, blatant, loud, or overt hostility or can be irritability, complaining (which is a combination of anger and helplessness), and even annoyance. Anger may sound irrational and can leave the bereaved feeling confused and/or guilty and doubting their mental health. Anger can take the form of pushing the helper away.

To deal with anger, find someone who can validate the angry feelings while supporting an appropriate expression of the anger.

Guilt and Shame

Guilt can lead to feelings of unworthiness, a desire to atone, self-punishment, and rejection of help from others. Guilt can focus on any part of the loss and need not be logical or realistic.

Guilt can result from the feeling that one should be omnipotent and so have prevented the loss. Guilt can also be induced by others out of their need to defend against their own painful feelings by blaming others for their loss.

Shame is the painful feeling that you have done something wrong, improper, or silly; a loss of reputation, disgrace, or dishonor. A person can feel there is something basically wrong with him or her that can't be fixed (which is not true).

Guilt is based on internalized parents. Shame is based on disapproval from outside. Guilt is wrong-doing. Shame is inferiority. Shame sets one apart; there's an unconscious fear of being abandoned. Guilt is fear of mutilation, connected to others. Shame sets off the wish to hide because one feels exposed. Guilt can be nullified by acts of atonement, confession, punishment, repentance, or expiation. Shame cannot be easily undone. It is a failure to live up to one's self expectations.

Defenses against shame are repression through denial, turning off emotionally, a direct attempt to correct the source of shame, conspiracy of silence, or blocking it out.

Guilt and shame need to be slowly expressed in the presence of an accepting, non-judgmental person so feelings can be integrated and restitution facilitated. Find someone who can educate you on guilt and shame and reassure you that your feelings are normal. Where guilt is induced by others, find help to see the source of the attack. The goal is to keep from feeling abandoned by having someone be understanding and empathic. Relief is experienced when you understand the legitimacy of your loss of trust in yourself, others, and the world.

Identification

This is the incorporation within the self of a mental picture of the lost person and then thinking, feeling, or acting as you conceive the person would do. So the bereaved try to be like their old self before the loss of body function or they try to be like the person they have lost.

Identification with the positive or idealized aspects of a person will increase one's self-esteem and help normal grieving. Identification with the fearful or hostile elements will result in guilt, shame, anxiety, and lowered self-esteem.

Identification can be in how you walk, facial expressions, interests, values or tastes of the lost person.

Identification is a holding on of the lost person/object internally.

Regression

This acting younger than your age can occur at the level of thoughts, feelings, defenses, or activity or in social relationships. One may regress in the type of relationship sought for in substitution for the one lost. Regression can allow time for the cultivation of inner resources—imagination, perception, and intellectual development.

Regression under stress, *if temporary*, can be both benign and functional. It allows one to go back to more familiar ways of being until equilibrium is restored, energy is renewed, and courage mobilized.

Suicidal fantasies may spring up at this time. They are usually a desire to escape from the pain. The bereaved should find someone to talk with about their fantasies, and the exploration will usually cut short the need to act them out. A person seriously planning suicide needs professional help immediately.

Helplessness and Depression

Helplessness is the feeling of being without the power to help oneself, being fearful or weak, feeling incompetent or inefficient.

Helplessness can be experienced as extremely painful. It can be a longing for the lost object/person and feeling helpless in facing the future without that object/person. Temporary helplessness in grief can serve to help a person survive and reattach to others.

The most direct solution to helplessness is dependency upon another person for mothering, love, affection, support, shelter, protection, security, food, etc. One can feel overwhelmed and therefore helpless by the amount of impulses and feelings they are having.

Helplessness needs to be experienced in order to recover from grief, but *don't push* anyone in or out too soon.

Helplessness is such a vulnerable feeling that any non-acceptance will shut it down. Caring, warmth, respect, empathy, hope, and an attempt to understand is needed by the bereaved. Find someone or several people who can support and help you as well as someone who can hear what you are experiencing in your grief.

Feelings of helplessness can be defended against by the bereaved by dumping them on others (i.e., "Yes, but . . .") or by attacking others. This will not move the bereaved through their grief process. They will become stuck.

Helplessness may also come out as depression. Those who avoid their feelings will get stuck in the grief process. Helplessness unsupported by a protective presence of another can lead to depression and hopelessness.

Hopelessness

Hopelessness is a feeling or belief that there is no hope. A common and easy defense is to withdraw into sleep. There are three stages (seen especially in children when separated from their mother) of emotional response to loss.

1. Protest due to the anxiety the person feels from the separation
2. Despair, which includes grief and mourning but develops into short-lived hopelessness
3. Emotional detachment, which occurs with inactivity and withdrawal. If this stage goes on too long the individual will give up and die.

Hope

Hope can be restored through a sense of industry. This sense develops out of mastering tasks that demand effort and struggle but are within the ability of the person. Hope continues when:

- tasks are taken in progression of difficulty,
- there are expectations of success by caring others, and
- there is a feeling of success by the bereaved.

If expectations are too high, this leads to excessive anxiety and feelings of hopelessness and failure.

The most common form of hopelessness is depression. Depressed people have flat affect (no expression in face, body, tone of voice, etc.). They have lost the capacity to have fun, and they dwell on what was lost. They feel prolonged inner emptiness. Helplessness in depression appears as indecisiveness, paralysis about action, increased demands on others, feelings of unworthiness, and guilt. They often project hopelessness on others so that those helping feel unable to be helpful. The ultimate expression of hopelessness is suicide.

There may be quick alterations between beginning a relationship and emotional turning off, depression, or hopelessness. Find someone who understands depression and grief and who can carry the hope for you with a firm, kind, and confident approach.

Phase 3: Integration of the loss and grief

Relief and Restoration of Meaning

Loss experienced as relief (of pain and suffering from lingering illness) can mean the positive memories are kept. Relief is intermingled with other emotions, such as anger, sadness, guilt, etc. Intermittent relief is beneficial to healthy mourning. In restoring meaning, there is a search for how and why they are suffering. Reasons for suffering need to be found. Try not to run away from the pain and grief, but move through it.

Restitution

This is a replacement of or a substitution for the lost object/person. Objects for restitution are both internal and external.

External

- Availability of acceptable replacement objects/persons/relationships
- Opportunities for experiences that raise self-esteem
- Timing of crucial events that help restore meaning

Internal restitution is affected by:

- Age of individual
- Health
- Personality
- Defenses
- Unconscious processes
- Flexibility
- State of energy

Material objects can become imbued with meaning through association with the lost object/person (significant people and memories) and are comforting. Dreams are a great source of mental restitution, as well as fantasy. They give the illusion that wishes have come true without looking at the obstacles. Hallucination and delusion can be attempts at restitution or retrieval and need professional help because they aren't helpful to functioning in the world or moving through the grief.

When restitution does not occur, depletion does.

Depletion

This is similar to burn-out or low gear. It can be set off by exhaustion at times. In depletion, goals are altered or abandoned, and there is partial or complete abandonment of external and internal reality. There is increased isolation and withdrawal of energy. When depletion improves, it moves to depression. A great deal of care and help is necessary, so find a professional who can help immediately.

Substitution can serve as an attempt at recovery but does not work.

Recovery from loss requires that:

1. Continuity be reestablished
2. Damaged self-esteem be repaired
3. A sense of meaning be restored

Reorganization within the life of the bereaved takes place partly in connection with the image of the lost object/person and partly in connection to new objects/persons.

UNLESS GRIEF IS WORKED THROUGH AND THE TIE BROKEN, THERE REMAINS EMOTIONAL ENERGY TIED TO THE LOST OBJECT/PERSON.

So find a professional that can help you through this process. Most of us were not allowed to have some part of this process growing up, and we need help to learn about it and move through it. Unresolved grief will create tension in the body and eventually the dis-ease will become disease.

Books, DVDs, Games, and Other Resources

Here is a list I compiled up to 2014 from my explorations in understanding high functioning autism, or Asperger's syndrome, and social communication disorder. They will all be helpful in working with those who have IRI.

Books

The following books are arranged by major category. Some books are listed more than once since they cover multiple issues.

Inductive Reasoning Issues

Anything from the following authors will be helpful in understanding and/or working with these those who have IRI.

- Dr. Tony Attwood was one of the first to write on Asperger's. His DVDs are great.
- Jed Baker clearly deals with issues in a great way for parents and teaches social skills to kids. He is the most accurate in understanding those with IRI.
- Michelle Garcia Winner is a speech therapist. She has many good books and workbooks for school or groups on teaching social skills. See www.SocialThinking.com.
- Carol Gray (The Gray Center for Social Learning) has several books on how to use social stories to help those who struggle with social skills and empathy. Using social stories helps them

understand how others may be thinking or feeling and how to respond appropriately to the person or situation.

- Carol Kranowitz (Out-of-Sync books) has books (and DVDs) on sensory issues of either too much input or not enough with many ideas on how to handle it.
- Temple Grandin has autism and is a visual thinker. She shares her insights and latest research up to 2013 in her newly published book.
- Ellen Notbohm has several good books on autism.
- Elizabeth Crary has great books on feelings and choices for dealing with them, whether the child struggles with IRI or not. She also has a parenting program.
- Jean Illsley Clarke has written great parenting books.

Sensory Issues

- *Starting Sensory Integration Therapy: Fun Activities that Won't Destroy Your Home or Classroom* by Bonnie Arnwine
- *Building Bridges through Sensory Integration* by Paula Aquilla, Shirley Sutton, and Ellen Yack
- *Answers to Questions Teachers Ask about Sensory Integration: Forms, Checklists, and Practical Tools* by Carol Kranowitz, Jane Koomar, and Stacey Szklut
- *Unlocking the Mysteries of Sensory Dysfunction* by Elizabeth Anderson and Pauline Emmons
- *The Sensory Connection: An OT and SLP Approach* by Nancy Kashman and Janet Mora
- *The Highly Sensitive Child or The Highly Sensitive Person* by Elaine Aron – not about autism but about those who can do empathy but are too sensitive; she has several books and online tests for children and adults at www.hsperson.com

- *The Goodenoughs Get in Sync* by Carol Kranowitz
- *Growing an In-Sync Child: Simple, Fun Activities to Help Every Child Develop, Learn, and Grow* by Carol Kranowitz and Joyce Newman
- Sensory solutions for the classroom by Carol Stock Kranowitz
    - *Preschool SENSE (Sensory Scan for Educators)* - manual and forms
    - *Answers to Questions Teachers Ask about Sensory Integration*
    - Learning in Motion
    - Move About Activity Cards by David Jereb, OTR/L, and Kathy Koehler, COTA/L

Asperger's Syndrome or Social Communication Disorder

- *The OASIS Guide to Asperger Syndrome: Completely Revised and Updated: Advice, Support, Insight, and Inspiration* by Patricia Romanowski Bashe, Barbara L. Kirby, Simon Baron-Cohen, and Tony Attwood – great for those newly diagnosed
- *The Complete Guide to Asperger's Syndrome* by Dr. Tony Attwood – great info but can be intimidating
- *Parenting Your Asperger Child: Individualized Solutions for Teaching Your Child Practical Skills* by Alan Sohn and Cathy Grayson – has great subtypes and cognitive behavioral ways to work with your child for each one.
- *Kids in the Syndrome Mix of ADHD, LD, Asperger's, Tourette's, Bipolar and More* by Martin L Kutscher, MD – short explanations, comparisons, and ideas for a variety of issues; covers basic meds and further reading. Nice resource!
- *All Cats Have Asperger Syndrome* by Kathy Hoopmann – good explanation of Asperger's syndrome for children

Temple Grandin Library

- *The Autistic Brain*
- *Emergence: Labeled Autistic* by Grandin and Margaret M. Scariano
- *Thinking in Pictures: and Other Reports from My Life with Autism*
- *The Way I See It: A Personal Look at Autism and Asperger's*
- *Unwritten Rules of Social Relationships: Decoding Social Mysteries through the Unique Perspectives of Autism*
- *Perspectives of Autism* by Temple Grandin and Sean Barron
- *A Thorn in My Pocket: Temple Grandin's Mother Tells the Family Story* by Eustacia Cutler
- *Developing Talents: Careers for Individuals with Asperger's Syndrome and High-functioning Autism*

From Those with Asperger's

- *Be Different* by John Elder Robison
- *Asperger's from the Inside Out: A Supportive and Practical Guide for Anyone with Asperger's Syndrome* by Michael John Carley
- *Pretending to Be Normal: Living With Asperger's Syndrome* by Liane Holliday Willey
- *Asperger's: What Does it Mean to Me?* by Catherine Faherty and Gary B. Mesibov
- *Mindblind* by Jennifer Rozines Roy
- *I Am Utterly Unique: Celebrating the Strengths of Children with Asperger Syndrome and High-Functioning Autism* by Elaine Marie Larson
- *Different Like Me: My Book of Autism Heroes* by Jennifer Elder

Parent Experience and Perspectives

These books can be helpful or frustrating depending on whether your child is like the author's child or not. There is something helpful in each book.

- *Hitchhiking through Asperger Syndrome* by Lise Pyles; great information and ideas from a mom's search and perspective, with three chapters on school
- *Life at the Edge and Beyond: Living with ADHD and Asperger Syndrome* by Jan Green; lower-functioning child (Level 3) who was home schooled
- *More Than a Mom: Living a Full and Balanced Life When Your Child Has Special Needs* by Amy Baskin and Heather Fawcett

Parenting

- *Parenting Your Asperger Child: Individualized Solutions for Teaching Your Child Practical Skills* by Alan Sohn and Cathy Grayson – has great subtypes and cognitive behavioral ways to work with your child for each one
- *Parenting a Child With Asperger Syndrome: 200 Tips and Strategies* by Brenda Boyd
- *Ten Things Every Child with Autism Wishes You Knew* by Ellen Notbohm
- *The Autism Trail Guide: Postcards from the Road Less Traveled* by Ellen Notbohm
- *More Than a Mom: Living a Full and Balanced Life When Your Child Has Special Needs* by Amy Baskin and Heather Fawcett
- *Understanding Your Child's Sensory Signals* by Angie Voss – identifies behaviors and ideas to help

Siblings & Friends

- *Autism through a Sister's Eyes* by Eve B. Band and Emily Hecht
- *Everybody Is Different: A Book for Young People Who Have Brothers or Sisters with Autism* by Fiona Bleach
- *The Autism Acceptance Book: Being a Friend to Someone with Autism* by Ellen Sabin
- Arthur books by Marc Brown including *Arthur and the New Kid*

School

- *Think Social: A Social Thinking Curriculum for School-Age Students* by Michelle Garcia Werner
- *School Success for Kids With Asperger's Syndrome: A Practical Guide for Parents and Teachers* by Stephan M. Silverman and Rich Weinfeld
- *Taming the Recess Jungle* by Carol Gray
- *Keeping a Head in School* by Mel Levine – for motivated students with a variety of learning issues, grades six through twelve
- *The Myth of Laziness* by Mel Levine – how kids and parents can become more productive with various stories from real life and how children were helped
- *Creating a Win-Win IEP for Students with Autism* by Beth Fouse
- *Inclusive Programming for Elementary Students with Autism* by Sheila Wagner
- *Ten Things Your Student with Autism Wishes You Knew* by Ellen Notbohm
- *1001 Great Ideas for Teaching and Raising Children with Autism or Asperger's* co-written by Veronica Zysk

- *Developing College Skills in Students with Autism and Asperger's Syndrome* by Sarita Freedman
- *Developing Talents: Careers for Individuals with Asperger Syndrome and High-functioning Autism* by Temple Grandin
- *Different Minds: Gifted children with AD/HD, Asperger Syndrome, and Other Learning Deficits* by Deirdre V. Lovecky
- *The Mislabeled Child: How Understanding Your Child's Unique Learning Style Can Open the Door to Success* by Brock Eide and Fernette Eide

Teens and Young Adults

- *Jarvis Clutch: Social Spy* by Mel Levine, Jarvis Clutch, and Ed Shems – great for any teen to help in understanding the various teen roles and how to fit in or not fit in if you choose
- *Uncommon Sense for Parents with Teenagers* by Michael Riera – explains what sixth through twelfth graders are dealing with developmentally; helps you to know what is neurotypical
- *Socially Curious and Curiously Social: A Social Thinking Guidebook for Teens & Young Adults with Asperger's, ADHD, PDD-NOS, NVLD, or Other Murky Undiagnosed Social Learning Issues* by Michelle Garcia Winner
- *A 5 Is Against the Law! Social Boundaries: Straight Up!* – an honest guide for teens and young adults by Kari Dunn Buron
- *Freaks, Geeks & Asperger Syndrome: A User Guide to Adolescence* by Luke Jackson
- *Social Skills Picture Book for High School and Beyond* by Dr. Jed Baker
- *Social Skills Training for Children and Adolescents with Asperger Syndrome and Social-Communications Problems* by Jed Baker
- *Your Life is Not a Label* by Jerry Newport

- *Autism-Asperger's and Sexuality* by Jerry and Mary Newport
- *Preparing for Life: The Complete Guide for Transitioning to Adulthood for Those with Autism and Asperger's Syndrome* by Dr. Jed Baker
- Asperger Syndrome and Adolescence: Practical Solutions for School Success by Brenda Smith Myles and Diane Adreon
- *Take Control of Asperger's Syndrome* by Janet Price and Jennifer Engel Fisher – understand your diagnosis, differences between NLD and AS, strategies to help you succeed in school and in friendships
- *Loving Mr. Spock* by Barbara Jacobs
- *Asperger's and Girls* by Tony Attwood, Temple Grandin, Teresa Bolick, Catherine Faherty, Lisa Iland, Jennifer McIlwee Myers, Ruth Snyder, Sheila Wagner, and Mary Wrobel
- *Aspergirls: Empowering Females with Asperger Syndrome* by Rudy Simone
- *Asperger's and Self-Esteem: Insight and Hope through Famous Role Models* by Norm Ledgin
- *Genius Genes: How Asperger Talents Changed the World* by Michael Fitzgerald and Brendan O'Brien

Sexuality

- *Intimate Relationships and Sexual Health: A Curriculum for Teaching Adolescents/Adults with High-Functioning Autism Spectrum Disorders and Other Social Challenges* by Catherine Davies and Melissa Dubie
- *Asperger's Syndrome and Sexuality: From Adolescence through Adulthood* by Isabelle Hénault
- *Taking Care of Myself: A Hygiene, Puberty, and Personal Curriculum for Young People with Autism* by Mary Wrobel

Couples

- *The Journal of Best Practices: A Memoir of Marriage, AS and one Man's Quest to be a Better Husband* by David Finch – humor and wisdom
- *The Other Half of Asperger Syndrome: A Guide to an Intimate Relationship with a Partner Who Has Asperger Syndrome* by Maxine C. Aston
- *Life with a Partner or Spouse with Asperger Syndrome: Going over the Edge? Practical Steps to Savings You and Your Relationship* by Kathy J. Marshack
- *Alone Together: Making an Asperger Marriage Work* by Katrin Bentley
- *Aspergers in Love: Couple Relationships and Family Affairs* by Maxine C. Aston
- *22 Things a Woman Must Know: If She Loves a Man with Asperger's Syndrome* by Rudy Simone
- *Love, Sex and Long-Term Relationships: What People with Asperger Syndrome Really Really Want* by Sarah Hendrickx
- *An Asperger Marriage* by Chris Slater-Walker and Gisela Slater-Walker

Alternative Therapies

- *Seeing through New Eyes: Changing the Lives of Children with Autism, Asperger Syndrome and Other Developmental Disabilities through Vision Therapy* by Melvin Kaplan
- *Disconnected Kids: The Groundbreaking Brain Balance Program for Children with Autism, ADHD, Dyslexia, and Other Neurological Disorders* by Dr. Robert Melillo
- *Cutting-Edge Therapies for Autism 2010–2011* by Ken Siri and Tony Lyons

- *A Child's Journey Out of Autism: One Family's Story of Living in Hope and Finding a Cure* by Leeann Whiffen
- *Smart Moves: Why Learning Is Not All in Your Head* by Carla Hannaford
- *The Healing Power of Neurofeedback: The Revolutionary LENS Technique for Restoring Optimal Brain Function* by Stephen Larsen
- *Energy Medicine* by Donna Eden

Health

- *Eating for Autism: the 10-Step Nutrition Plan* by Elizabeth Strickland
- *Children with Starving Brains: A Medical Treatment Guide for Autism Spectrum Disorder* by Jaquelyn McCandless – digestive issues, absorption, toxins, etc.
- *Enzymes for Autism and Other Neurological Conditions* by Karen DeFelice – good explanation of the digestion system and their personal journey
- *Brainmaker: The Power of Gut Microbes to Heal and Protect Your Brain* by David Permutter, MD – great book for understanding how good gut bacteria affects all your body including the brain. This one is for everyone!
- *Prescriptions for Nutritional Healing* by Phyllis A Balch. A practical A-Z reference to drug-free remedies using vitamins, minerals, herbs and food supplements.
- *The LCP Solution: The Nutritional Treatment for ADHD, Dyslexia, and Dyspraxia* by B. Jacqueline Stordy, PhD – explains the importance of Omega-3s, zinc, and magnesium and the research behind improvements in the listed disorders

- *Just Take a Bite: Easy, Effective Answers to Food Aversions and Eating Challenges* by Dr. Lori Ernsperger and Tania Stegen-Hanson
- *A Drug-free Approach to Asperger Syndrome and Autism: Homeopathic Care for Exceptional Kids* by by Judyth Reichenberg-Ullman, Robert Ullman, Ian Luepker, and Bernard Rimland
- *Healing the New Childhood Epidemics: Autism, ADHD, Asthma, and Allergies: The Groundbreaking Program for the 4-A Disorders* by Kenneth Bock and Cameron Stauth
- *The Autism & ADHD Diet: A Step-by-Step Guide to Hope and Healing by Living Gluten Free and Casein Free (GFCF) and Other Interventions* by Barrie Silberberg
- *Special-Needs Kids Eat Right: Strategies to Help Kids on the Autism Spectrum Focus, Learn, and Thrive* by Judy Converse
- *Changing the Course of Autism: A Scientific Approach for Parents and Physicians* by Bryan Jepson and Jane Johnson
- *Special Diets for Special Kids* by Lisa Lewis
- *Nourishing Hope for Autism: Nutrition Intervention for Healing Our Children* by Julie Matthews
- *Healing and Preventing Autism: A Complete Guide* by Jenny McCarthy and Dr. Jerry Kartzinel
- *Adrenal Fatigue: The 21st Century Stress Syndrome* by James L Wilson, ND, DC, PhD – not specific to IRI but due to the levels of stress I included it and
- *The Adrenal Reset Diet* by Alan Christianson, MD
- The *Ultimate pH Solution* by Michelle Schoffro Cook – great understanding of how the body functions and the importance of pH balance for everyone

Behavioral Issues - General

- *Power Cards: Using Special Interests to Motivate Children and Youth with Asperger Syndrome and Autism* by Elisa Gagnon
- *A Treasure Chest of Behavior Strategies for Individuals with Autism* by Beth Fouse and Maria Wheeler

Anger

- *No More Meltdowns* by Jed Baker
- *Asperger Syndrome and Difficult Moments: Practical Solutions for Tantrums, Rage and Meltdowns* by Brenda Smith Myles and Jack Southwick
- *My Book Full of Feelings: How to Control and React to the Size of Your Emotions* by Amy Jaffe and Luci Gardner
- *A "5" Could Make Me Lose Control! An activity-based method for evaluating and supporting highly anxious students* by Kari Dunn Buron
- *Sadness and Anger* by Dr. Tony Attwood
- The Way to A: Empowering Children with Autism Spectrum and Other Neurological Disorders to Monitor and Replace Aggression and Tantrum Behavior by Hunter Manasco

Anxiety

- *When My Worries Get Too Big! A Relaxation Book for Children Who Live with Anxiety* by Kari Dunn Buron
- *Asperger Syndrome and Anxiety: A Guide to Successful Stress Management* by Nick Dubin
- *The Relaxation and Stress Reduction Workbook* by Martha Davis, Elizabeth Robbins Eshelman, and Matthew McKay – good for anyone

Social skills

These books are for working with a variety of ages.

- *Navigating the Social World* by Jeanie McAfee
- *Thinking about YOU thinking about ME* by Michelle Garcia Winner – see all her books on www.SocialThinking.com
- *Social Thinking at Work* by Michelle Garcia Winner
- *Unwritten Rules of Social Relationships: Decoding Social Mysteries through the Unique Perspectives of Autism* by Temple Grandin and Sean Barron
- *Social Skills Training for Children and Adolescents with Asperger Syndrome and Social-Communications Problems* by Jed E. Baker, Ph.D.
- *The Social Skills Picture Book Teaching play, emotion, and communication to children with autism* by Jed Baker; also a CD-ROM (containing all images from the book) for younger children
- *Comic Strip Conversations* by Carol Gray – teaches how to develop social stories to help teach kids social skills
- *The New Social Story Book* by Carol Gray – 150 social stories and CD-ROM
- *My Social Stories Book* by Carol Gray and Abbie White with three chapters: "Taking Care of Me," "Home," and "Going Places for 3-8 Year Olds"
- *Incredible 5-Point Scale: Assisting Students with Autism Spectrum Disorders in Understanding Social Interactions and Controlling Their Emotional Responses* by Kari Dunn Buron and Mitzi Curtis
- *The Hidden Curriculum: Practical Solutions for Understanding Unstated Rules in Social Situations* by Brenda Smith Myles, Melissa L. Trautman, and Rhonda L. Schelvan – explanation of it, teaching, it and curriculum items

- *Social Skills for Teenagers and Adults with Asperger Syndrome: A Practical Guide to Day-to-day Life* by Nancy J. Patrick
- *Teaching Your Child the Language of Social Success* by Marshall P. Duke, Stephen Nowicki Jr., and Elisabeth A. Martin
- *Helping the Child Who Doesn't Fit In* by Stephen Nowicki and Marshall P. Duke
- *Good Friends Are Hard to Find: Help Your Child Find, Make and Keep Friends* by Fred H. Frankel (illustrated by Barry Wetmore)
- *The Social Success Workbook for Teens: Skill-building Activities for Teens with Nonverbal Learning Disorder, Asperger's Disorder, and Other Social-skill Problems* by Barbara Cooper and Nancy Widdows
- *Playing It Right! Social Skills Activities for Parents and Teachers of Young Children with Autism Spectrum Disorders, Including Asperger Syndrome and Autism* by Rachael Bareket
- *Teaching Children with Autism to Mind-Read: A Practical Guide* by Patricia Howlin, Simon Baron-Cohen, and Julie Hadwin
- *Teach Me Language: A Language Manual for Children with Autism, Asperger's Syndrome and Related Developmental Disorders* by Sabrina Freeman, PhD and Lorelei Dake – not just for non-verbal children; helpful for teaching concepts from friendship to grammar, letter and word problems, and more

The Brain

These books are not specific to autism, Aspeger's, etc. They are about brain function and learning that can be helpful.

- *A Mind at a Time* and *The Myth of Laziness* by Mel Levine
- *The Woman Who Changed Her Brain* by Barbara Arrowsmith Young

- *Mindsight, The Whole-Brain Child* and *Brainstorm* by Daniel J. Siegel
- *The Brain That Changes Itself* and *The Brain's Way of Healing* by Norman Doidge

Children's Books with Social Themes

These are good for any child of Preschool/Kindergarten through Early Elementary Ages whether they can do inductive reasoning or not.

Dealing with Feelings

- *I'm Mad* by Elizabeth Crary
- *I'm Frustrated* by Elizabeth Crary
- *I'm Proud* by Elizabeth Crary
- *I'm Furious* by Elizabeth Crary
- *I'm Excited* by Elizabeth Crary
- *When I Feel Angry* by Cornelia Maude Spelman
- *Andrew's Angry Words* by Dorthea Lachner
- *The Feelings Book* by Todd Parr
- *But I Want It* by Dr. Laura Schlessinger

Solving Social Problems

- *I Want It* by Elizabeth Crary
- *I Want to Play* by Elizabeth Crary
- *My Name Is Not Dummy* by Elizabeth Crary
- *I'm Lost* by Elizabeth Crary
- *I Can't Wait* by Elizabeth Crary
- *Mommy, Don't Go* by Elizabeth Crary

Dealing with Bullying/Teasing

- *The Berenstain Bears and the Bully* by Stan and Jan Berenstain
- *Simon's Hook: A Story about Teases and Put-downs* by Karen Gedig Burnett
- *Nobody Knew What to Do: A Story about Bullying* by Becky Ray McCain
- *Stand Tall, Molly Lou Melon* by Patty Lovell, WPS
- *Bobby and Mandee's Too Smart for Bullies* by Robert Kahn and Sharon Chandler
- *Just a Bully* by Mercer Mayer

Friendship Skills

- *Join In and Play* by Cheri J. Meiners
- *Feeling Left Out* by Kate Petty and Charlotte Firmin
- *Will I Have a Friend?* by Miriam Cohen
- *My Friends and Me: A First Look at Friendship* by Pat Thomas
- *Enemy Pie* by Derek Munson
- *Nobody Likes Me* by Raoul Krischanitz
- *Be a Friend* by Regina Burch
- *How to Be a Friend* by Laurie Krasny Brown and Marc Brown
- *Friends* by Helme Heine
- *Tobin Learns to Make a Friend* by Diane Murrell
- *Being Friends* by Karen Beumont, WPS
- *We Can Get Along* by Lauren Murphey Payne

Learning about Rules

- *The Tale of Peter Rabbit* by Beatrix Potter

Sharing

- *Two Can Share Too* by Janelle Cherrington
- *Pooh, I Can Share Too* by Caoline Kenneth
- *Care Bears: The Day Nobody Shared* by Nancy Parent
- *It's My Turn* by David Bedford and Elaine Fiela
- *Share and Take Turns* by Cheri J. Meiners

Listening

- *Listen Buddy* by Helen Lester
- *Listen and Learn* by Cheri J. Meiners

Dealing with Being Different

- *Odd Velvet* by Mary E. Whitcomb
- *It's Okay to Be Different* by Todd Parr

Other Social Skills

- *The Berenstain Bears Learn All about Strangers* by Stan and Jan Berenstain
- *The Berenstain Bears Get the Gimmies* by Stan and Jan Berenstain
- *The Berenstain Bears and the Trouble with Friends* by Stan and Jan Berenstain
- *The Berenstain Bears Forget Their Manners* by Stan and Jan Berenstain
- *Franklin's New Friend* by Helene Heine
- *A Kid's Guide to Making Friends* by Joy Wilt
- *Understand and Care* by Cheri J. Meiners
- *Blabber Mouse* by True Kelly (for ages five to ten)
- *Too Safe for Strangers* by Robert Kahn

- *The Real Winner* by Charise Neugebauer (about cooperation)
- *People Say Hello* by Will Barber
- *Let's Talk About* series of books by Joy Berry

DVDs, Other Recordings, Movies, and TV

- *Navigating the Social World* DVD by Jeanie McAfee – great beginning one
- *Dr. Tony Attwood presents: Asperger's Diagnostic and Assessment* DVD
- *Asperger's Syndrome, Vol. 1 DVD: A Guide for Parents and Professionals* by Dr. Tony Attwood – great info and easier than the book unless reading is your style
- *Asperger's Syndrome, Vol. 2 DVD: Anger Management, Teaching Teachers, and Teenage Issues* by Dr. Tony Attwood – again great info
- *Social Skills Training and Frustration Management* DVD, by Dr. Jed Baker, Temple Grandin, and Sean Barron
- *Writing Social Stories with Carol Gray* DVD and accompanying booklet
- *Exploring Feelings DVD: Cognitive Behavior Therapy to Manage Anxiety* by Dr. Tony Attwood
- *Model Me Kids*, videos for learning social skills, student workbooks and teaching manuals, www.ModelMeKids.com
- *TD Social Skills*, well-done videos on social skills; TDSocialSkills.com
- *Normal People Scare Me* by Joey Travolta; his explanation and personal experiences
- *The Way I See It: A Video Presentation by Dr. Temple Grandin* – her experiences

- *Autism and Asperger's Syndrome: An Insightful Presentation* DVD by Dr. Temple Grandin

Social Skills

- www.ModelMeKids.com – has several good DVDs for kids 2–17, along with teaching manuals and student workbooks
- www.TDSocialSkills.com – has several good DVDs that show kids having an interaction, then with what they are thinking before responding, and then how to respond in ways that build the relationship; also has an Emotional Empowerment System using cards to think through and manage emotions.
- *My School Day*, available through www.socialskillbuilder.com, includes modules for lunch, recess, classroom, hallway, etc. For each module, there are four levels: level 1 is a video clip of real children and situations, level 2 is multiple choice, level 3 is interactive (e.g., click on body parts that tell you she is listening, etc.), and level 4 is question and answer. Topics include listening, following directions, waiting your turn, walking quietly in the hall, joining in play, teasing, etc.
- Mind Reading, learn to identify facial expressions and emotions, Future Horizons
- *The Social Skills Picture Book Teaching Play, Emotion, and Communication to Children with Autism* by Jed Baker CD-ROM containing all images from the book of the same name for younger children
- *The New Social Story Book* by Carol Gray – 150 social stories and CD-ROM

Anger

- *Exploring Feelings: Cognitive Behavior Therapy to Manage Anger* DVD by Dr. Tony Attwood
- *Asperger's Syndrome Vol. 2* DVD by Tony Attwood – anger management, teaching teachers, and teenage issues

Sensory Issues

- Carol Kranowitz Library – DVDs (in addition to her books) with lots of great ideas on working with children who lack sensory input or are overwhelmed by it, exercises for each sense, fine motor coordination, oral-motor, motor planning, etc.
    - *The Out-of-Sync Child* DVD
    - *Sensory Issues in Learning & Behavior* DVD
    - *Getting Kids in Sync* DVD
- *Sensory Challenges and Answers* DVD by Dr. Temple Grandin
- Sensory solutions for the classroom by Carol Stock Kranowitz
    - *Preschool SENSE (Sensory Scan for Educators)* - manual and forms
    - *Answers to Questions Teachers Ask about Sensory Integration*
    - *Teachers Ask about Sensory Integration* CD
    - *Sensory Issues in Learning & Behavior* DVD

Movies

The following blog lists movies, some of which involve someone with high-functioning autism/Asperger's/social communication disorder: aspiegirls.wordpress.com/2012/12/28/2-movies-where-one-or-more-character-got-autism-or-aspergers/.

TV

- The Big Bang Theory
- Community
- Parenthood
- Scorpion
- Doc Martin
- The top ten TV characters that have Asperger's syndrome characteristics are listed on www.dailykos.com/story/2013/01/12/1178226/-Top-10-Apparently-Asperger-Characters-in-Film-TV.

Social Skills Games

There is an increasing number of games available. Keep checking back at various websites listed below for the new ones.

Board Games

- Franklin Learning Systems has a storefront on Amazon with a lot of games for social skills and pragmatic language skills including Escape From Anger Island, Friendship Island, Bullies to Buddies, True Friends, Circle of Respect, etc.
- Family Pastimes cooperative board games. All of their games are about working together to meet goals and include:
    - Sleeping Grump (ages 4–7)
    - The Secret Door (ages 5 and up)
    - Snowstorm (ages 5 and up)
    - Granny's House (ages 4–7)

- Berthold Berg, PhD, has several books with workbooks, story, and some with DVDs including:
    - The Anger Control Game,
    - The Bullying Game
    - The Self Concept Game
    - The Social Conflict Game
    - The Social Skills Game
- Barbara Sher has some helpful books on games (ages 3–12) including:
    - *Early Intervention Games: Fun, Joyful Ways to Develop Social and Motor Skills in Children with Autism Spectrum or Sensory Processing Disorders*
    - Social, Motor and Sensory Games
- LinguiSystems (www.LinguiSystems.com) has many games for various learning issues. They give a good list of ages and quick synopsis of what they carry. Any theory of mind, questions, inferences are all good for teaching social skills including:
    - Maxwell's Manor (ages 4–9)
    - Friendzee (ages 7–11)
    - The Emotions Game (ages 5–12)
    - No Glamour Social Language/Behavior Cards (ages 5–11)
    - The Non-Verbal Language Kit (ages 7–16)
    - That's Life: A Game of Social Language (ages 12–16)

- Super Duper Publications' website, www.SuperDuperInc.com, has many games for various learning issues. They have a search engine for topic, age, price, etc. Enter "social skills" under topic, and you will get several games, including:
    - Ask and Answer Social Skills Game
    - Mind Your Manners Social Skills Game
    - Socially Speaking Game
    - Practicing Pragmatics Fun Deck
- Creative Therapy Store's website, www.CreativeTherapyStore.com, has some games and books for several diagnoses, including autism and Asperger's.
- Communicate Junior (grades 1–4), use with Social Star Books 1–3; Thinking Publications Communicate (grades 4 and up), use with SSS: Social Skills Strategies Books A and B, Thinking Publications
- Move About Activity Cards by David Jereb, OTR/L, and Kathy Koehler, COTA/L
- Amazon carries a lot if you know the titles. Look for:
    - Totika games on topics such as life skills, self-esteem, beliefs, etc.
    - Talk Blocks by Innovative Interactions
    - Bully Buster Bingo
    - Too Much, Too Little, Just Right: A Social Communication Game by Claudia Weiss, LCSW, Sandra Singer, PhD, and Lois Feigenbaum, LCSW
    - Angry Animals 2: A Board Game Teaching Healthy Expression of Anger by Katelyn Mariah (ages 5–12)

- WPS has several games including:
    - Psymon by Eric B. Vogel – Psy.D Kids love collecting cards, and they'll love capturing Psymon cards as they learn important cognitive-behavioral skills with this enchanting board game.
    - Clue Cards: 5 Card Packs to Improve Social Communication
    - Peacetown: A Conflict Resolution Game (ages 7–12)
    - The Peace Path (ages 6–14)
    - The Changing Family Game and Workbook –focuses on divorce
    - Use Your I's by Donna McGoff – teaches children how to express feelings

Online Games

- www.do2learn.com – has games that teach about facial expressions and feelings
- www.quia.com – has a game that teaches about feelings
- Team Asperger's www.ccoder.com/GainingFace/ – identifies facial features, compares different expressions, and has a quiz you can take
- www.ICanDoApps.com – apps for emotions, associations, inferences, etc.; iPhone and iPad apps for speech and language development

Online Resources

These websites have good books and/or games for learning about and teaching social skills.

- www.FreeSpirit.com – Free Spirit Publishers
- www.fhautism.com – Future Horizon
- www.jkp.com – Jessica Kingsley Publishers
- www.SocialThinking.com – has lots of books and resources, especially for teachers
- www.SocialSkillBuilder.com – many CDs with books
- www.SuperDuperInc.com – Super Duper Publications
- www.AutismSpeaks.org – information and resources for those with high-functioning to highly impacted autism; see particularly www.autismspeaks.org/family-services/tool-kits/asperger-syndrome-and-high-functioning-autism-tool-kit
- www.acadcom.com – has some resources for those with moderate to highly affected autism
- www.DiffLearn.com – Different Roads has many DVDs and teaching tools mostly for those with highly impacted, but some can help high-functioning children
- www.autism.org – National Autistic Society (Australia) has books for all ages on the spectrum

Worksheets and Instructions

Filling Out the Worksheets

The worksheets are designed to help you organize information that you figure out as you read through the book. It is a way to help you share information between those of you that have IRI and those that don't if both are ready to talk about IRI. This book is not designed to help you resolve conflicts or frustrations, or past resentments and hurts. It is not meant to be used to make someone believe he or she has IRI. It is not meant to be used in anger or frustration ever. Please get help from a psychotherapist if those feelings keep occurring and aren't resolved. Please remember that those who have IRI usually are not trying to be hurtful. Because they have IRI, they don't understand how their thoughts or behavior will affect you.

Fill out the worksheets as you read the book. If you have finished reading it already, you can go back and review it quickly and fill out the sheet. If there is more than one person with IRI in the family, review and fill out worksheets for each person.

Levels

Mark the level overall that you think you or the person with IRI is at. You may not be clear about this until you go through some or all the aspects. That's OK. Just come back and do it at the end. Or you can guess now and then see if you agree with yourself at the end.

Level 2 are those who are totally unaware that they have an aspect. They will accept that they do if a person of authority tells them. They may not have much motivation to change, other than to do what they are told. They will have no idea how to work on it unless they are told specifics. They will do exactly what they are told to do without any adaptation to a person or situation unless they are taught about that. They may easily forget in a new situation to do what they have been told in the past.

Level 2+ are those who often remember to do exactly what they are told. They won't know how to adapt to a new person or situation without a lot of coaching. They will have no personal motivation to work on the aspect, except to obey their authority figure.

Level 3- are those that have an idea they have difficulty with an aspect. They have some personal motivation to work on the aspect at least some of the time with some people that are important to them. They don't know what to do unless they are told. They will follow instructions exactly but may need reminders at times.

Level 3 can easily understand that they have difficulty with an aspect. They will follow instructions exactly and usually remember them but may need occasional reminders. They will quickly adapt their behavior when reminded. They are motivated to work on aspects, especially if they are told how it will benefit them and if they are an extrovert who needs more people contact.

Level 3+ know they have difficulty with an aspect but don't know what to do. They may tell others about it if they are an extrovert, so that others don't expect too much of them. Once they get help, they will seek information from that person in order to function better. They will adapt old information to new situations with regular coaching.

Level 4- know they have difficulty with an aspect but usually don't want others to know they are struggling. They will mimic their peers to avoid standing out and may respond a little slowly. They may or may not understand things once they think about it. They have personal motivation to work on aspects once they know whom to talk to and how to work on them. They will rarely need reminders.

Level 4 easily learn how to adapt to new situations or people with coaching. They are highly motivated to learn and be socially appropriate. They will struggle to understand others, but they will accept what they are told by their chosen helper or authority figure. They will ask questions easily if they trust that person.

Introvert vs. Extrovert

Now mark how much of an introvert or extrovert you or the person with IRI is. Remember that *extroverts generally gain energy by being around people.* They tend to process verbally with others when they are trying to figure something out or deal with their feelings. *Introverts are sucked dry energetically by being around others.* They need time alone to process information. Being alone rejuvenates them.

High introverts don't talk much. They will answer questions when asked directly. They tend to want to spend time with only one person at a time and often only family. They need more alone time than most in order to recover from any social situation or multiple-person situation. They need alone time in order to figure out what they think, feel, need, or want.

Moderate introverts will talk a little more. They may choose occasional social situations with people that are important to them, including family. They still need more alone time than most in order to recover from any social situation or multiple-person situation. They need alone time in order to figure out what they think, feel, need, or want.

Low introverts will talk with others fairly often. They will choose to spend some time with others that are important to them, including family. They listen a lot to others who are important to them. They need more alone time than people time to recover. They still need time alone to figure out their thoughts, feelings, needs, or wants.

Low extroverts will tend to spend some time with people. At times they will need to talk with others to figure out what they think, feel, need, or want. They will need some alone time to relax and recover. They listen a lot to others who are important to them.

Moderate extroverts will spend time with others regularly. They will seek social situations with friends and family. They will often need to talk with others to figure out what they think, feel, need, or want.

High extroverts will need or want to talk a lot. They will want to share all the details of their day, all their feelings and thoughts. They struggle to listen well to others unless coached. They will talk with anyone, including strangers, and may need coaching on who is safe or appropriate. They will need to talk with others to figure out what they think, feel, need, or want.

Feeler vs. Thinker

Now determine whether you or the person with IRI is a Thinker or a Feeler and how strongly you or the person has that trait. Language is a clue. If someone often says, "I feel that . . .," that person is a Feeler even though he or she is stating a thought with that sentence. If someone generally says, "I think that . . .," the person is usually a Thinker. You can also use the Myers Briggs Type Indicator or the Keirsey Bates shortened inventory from *Please Understand Me* to determine this.

Strong Feelers will tend to react with feelings overtly most of the time. They will have to address their feelings before they can address their thoughts. They may feel as if their feelings run them instead of having the control. They may struggle to identify thoughts that led to their feelings.

Moderate Feelers will tend to react with feelings overtly but can stop themselves in the process and think about them with coaching. They will identify their thoughts behind the feeling once they learn how to do it.

Low Feelers will tend to react with feelings a little more often than with thoughts. They often quickly recognize both their thoughts and feelings.

Low Thinkers will tend to react with thoughts a little more than feelings. They can quickly recognize both their thoughts and feelings.

Moderate Thinkers will respond with thoughts and with some coaching will identify feelings they have about their thoughts.

Strong Thinkers will respond with thoughts and struggle to identify their feelings. They may not know the importance of feelings unless they are taught. Even with coaching, it will take them a while to identify their feelings. Or they may need to come back to a conversation later once they have more time to figure them out.

Aspects of Inductive Reasoning

Now go through each of the aspects in chapter two and determine which ones you think apply. Different aspects can have different levels. Choose a level of impact for that aspect. Give one to two examples of what you have seen that support your best guess. Use the back of the aspects worksheets if needed.

Overall IRI Level Worksheet

Name of the writer____

Person with IRI____

(Write the name if it's not you and you want to remember whom this is about; otherwise, leave blank to keep confidentiality.)

Overall Level of Functioning

2 2+ 3- 3 3+ 4- 4

Introvert

|--------------------------|--------------------------|--------------------------|

Rarely talks Watches others a lot Spends most time alone Processes on his/her own	Talks some Watches others a lot Spends a lot of time alone Processes mostly on his/her own	Talks 40-60% Watches others a lot Spends some time with others Processes some with others

Feeler

|--------------------------|--------------------------|--------------------------|

Reacts without being aware of his/her thoughts that led to the feelings. Needs coaching to access his/her thoughts.	Feeling-oriented but can stop and go back and figure out his/her thoughts that led to the feelings, especially with coaching.	Can access both own feelings and own thoughts. Still tends to be a thinker when expressing himself/herself.

I think my self, partner, son, daughter, parent, sibling, client, student, grandparent, grandchild, nephew, niece, aunt, uncle, other ____________________________
(circle the relationship to you) has IRI.

Continuums

Mark on the continuum lines the level of introvert or extrovert and the level of feeler or thinker.

Extrovert

---|---|

Talks 50-70% of the time Watches others some Spends half of time with others Processes mostly with others when others will listen	Talks as much as allowed with others Spends more than half his/her time with others if allowed Processes aloud with or without others around

Thinker

---|---|

Mostly thinks about things. Given time and some coaching on defining feelings, can access the feelings he/she has about own thoughts. Often struggles to identify others' feelings.	Only thinks about things and has great difficulty identifying own or others' feelings. With coaching, very slowly begins to identify own feelings about his/her thoughts.

IRI Aspects Worksheet Date________________________

Level Aspect

1. _____ Body Language
2. _____ Eye Contact
3. _____ Body Language of Others
4. _____ Body Awareness of Self
5. _____ Making Meaning
6. _____ Translating Meaning to Other Situations
7. _____ Grouping Similar Things
8. _____ Empathy
9. _____ Understanding and Caring about Others
10. _____ Their Impact on Others
11. _____ Learning from Past Experiences
12. _____ Initiating
13. _____ Asking for Help
14. _____ Literal
15. _____ Perfectionist
16. _____ Resistance to Change–Possible OCD
17. _____ Imagination
18. _____ Memory

Attention

19. _____ Attending
20. _____ Planning
21. _____ Organization
22. _____ Monitoring Self
23. _____ Time Awareness
24. _____ Over Focus
25. _____ Lack of Focus

Mega-rules, Rules, and Sub-rules

26. _____ Uses Rules
27. _____ Creates Own Rules

Person with IRI____________________________

Example(s)

1. ____________________________
2. ____________________________
3. ____________________________
4. ____________________________
5. ____________________________
6. ____________________________
7. ____________________________
8. ____________________________
9. ____________________________
10. ____________________________
11. ____________________________
12. ____________________________
13. ____________________________
14. ____________________________
15. ____________________________
16. ____________________________
17. ____________________________
18. ____________________________

Attention

19. ____________________________
20. ____________________________
21. ____________________________
22. ____________________________
23. ____________________________
24. ____________________________
25. ____________________________

Mega-rules, Rules, and Sub-rules

26. ____________________________
27. ____________________________

Use the back of the sheet for additional explanation on the examples.

IRI Aspects Worksheet Date______________________

Level Aspect

Feelings

28. _____ Mad
29. _____ Sad
30. _____ Glad
31. _____ Scared
32. _____ Stress
33. _____ Worry
34. _____ Fear
35. _____ Anxiety
36. _____ Panic
37. _____ Frustration
38. _____ Depression
39. _____ Confused

Coping & Communication

40. _____ Gaming
41. _____ Taking on a Role
42. _____ Using Down Time
43. _____ Communication
44. _____ Understands Colloquialisms and Idioms

Sensory Overload or Lack of Filters

45. _____ See
46. _____ Hear
47. _____ Touch
48. _____ Taste
49. _____ Smell

Over-stimulating Environments Calmed by

50. _____ Color
51. _____ Sound
52. _____ Texture
53. _____ Temperature
54. _____ Other Aspect______________________
55. _____ Other Aspect______________________

Person with IRI____________________________

Example(s)

Feelings

28. ________________________________
29. ________________________________
30. ________________________________
31. ________________________________
32. ________________________________
33. ________________________________
34. ________________________________
35. ________________________________
36. ________________________________
37. ________________________________
38. ________________________________
39. ________________________________

Coping & Communication

40. ________________________________
41. ________________________________
42. ________________________________
43. ________________________________
44. ________________________________

Sensory Overload or Lack of Filters

45. ________________________________
46. ________________________________
47. ________________________________
48. ________________________________
49. ________________________________

Over-stimulating Environments Calmed by

50. ________________________________
51. ________________________________
52. ________________________________
53. ________________________________
54. ________________________________
55. ________________________________

Use the back of the sheet for additional explanation on the examples.

Index

ADD, x, xii, 15, 158, 170
ADHD, x, xii
  diagnosis, 158, 170
  extroverts, 13
  lack of focus, 86–87, 131
  sensory seeker, 141
  shock and, 195
adjustment disorder, 157
adults/young adults with IRI, 79, 86, 88, 117, 178–179
  books for, 219–220
alternative therapies, books, 221–222
ambivalence, stage of grief, 204
Amen, Daniel, ADD categories (*Healing ADD*), 170
American Speech-Language-Hearing Association, 163
analog time clock, 83
anger
  books topic, 224
  in grieving, 205
anxiety, x, xii, 35, 68, 85, 99, 100–101, 103, 105, 112, 134, 140, 141, 169
  books, 224
anxiety disorder diagnosis, 158, 170
apologizing, 185
Aron, Elaine, www.hsperson.com, 143
Arrowsmith Young Barbara, 149
Asperger's syndrome, x
  attention, 75, 80
  books, 215, 216
  causes, 147
  diagnosis, 3, 158, 170
  tests, 164–165
audiotaping instructions, 76
autism/autism spectrum, x, xii
  causes, 147, 149, 158
  DAN! doctors for, 193
  diagnostic tools, 170
  dyspraxia, 142
  imagination, lack, 69
  mental health counselors for, 190
  postural disorders, 141
autism/autism spectrum (*continued*)
  sensory discrimination, 142
  sensory overload, 131
  single focus, 5
  tests, 164–165
  under-responsibility, 141

Baker, Jed, books, 92, 213
behaviors
  books, 224
  expectations, 128
  indicating IRI, 2–3
  issues, 91–92
  negative, 177
bipolar, xii
  diagnosis, 158, 170
  extroverts, 13
  memory issues, 73
  shock and, 195–196
body awareness, 31, 35–36. *See also* relaxation methods
  of self, 31–33
body function issues, 166
body language/body and facial cues, 31, 42
  of IRI, 30, 31–33, 123
  reading others, 30–31, 42, 113
  and safety, 144–145
  social skills training , 30
books. *See also* DVDs, movies, TV
  alternative therapies, 221–222
  Asperger's syndrome, 215, 216
  autism, 216
  behavioral – anger, anxiety, social skills, 224–226
  brain, 216, 226–227
  children's, 227–230
  couples, 221
  health, 222–223
  inductive reasoning issues, 213–214
  parents/parenting, 217
  school, 218–219
  sensory issues, 214–215
  sexuality, 220–221

books (*continued*)
siblings and friends, 218
social communication disorder, 215
teens and young adults, 219–220
bosses, expectations and understanding of IRI, xi
boundaries, invading/setting, 93, 144
brain
books, 216, 226–227
-body connections/disconnect, 34, 54
chemicals/hormones, 148
developing, 138
and diagnostic criteria, 157, 170
different in everyone, 25, 65, 147
down time/rest, 125
filters, and lack of, 130–131
flexible, 149
fMRI and SPECT scans, 149
function and functional disorders, 147
lack of inductive reasoning, 45, 46, 79
neurologist as therapist, 193
over focus, 84, 85
during puberty, 81, 114
reflex development, 130–131
reinforcement control, 79
rules, prioritizing, 89
sensory pathways, 130–131
toxicity exposure, 110, 154
trauma, 148–149, 157–158
working memory, 72, 73
Brain Gym/educational kinesiology, 35–36, 134, 139 , 140, 197
Brain Maker (David Perlmutter, MD), 109
breathing for relaxation, 34–35, 36
bullying/teasing books, 228

calendar
keeping, 76
weekly, in layers, 82–83
calming techniques, 35
Candless, Jacquelyn (*Children with Starving Brains*), 110
caring for others, encouraging, 45–47
cell phone or handheld recorder as useful, 76, 77
change, resistance,67– 69
children/youth/teens with IRI, xi, 11, 45, 55, 56, 177–178, 184
asking for help, 58–60
behavior expectations, 128
books with social themes, 227–230
brain trauma, 148
chores, 117–118
coaching, 70
depression, 112
down time, 122–123, 124
elementary school work, checking for direction following, 57
L4s, 59–60
notebook for their use, 58–59
parents working with, 87
psychotherapist help, 59, 123
sensitivity to taste and smell, 133
setting priorities, 80
technology and gaming, 71
Children with Starving Brains (McCandless and Zimmerman), 110
Clarke, Jean Illsley, 92, 214
coaches/working with those with IRI, 41, 70, 191
cognitive behavioral therapy (CBT), 196
colloquialisms, 128–129, 130, 175, 185
communication. *See also* meaning, making and translating
and cultural expectations, 128
difficulties, 15
with IRI person, 38, 46, 53
and miscommunication, 126–127
patience from IRI person, 41
at puberty, 114
questioning successfully, 127
specificity required, 41, 125
successful, 127
conversations, initiating, 55–56
Cook, Michelle Schoffro (*Ultimate pH Solution*), 151
coping methods/skills/tools, 68, 69, 84, 105, 117
previewing, 77
at puberty, 114
therapy, 194
couples, books, 221
Counsel-Heal.com. *See* www. Counsel-Heal.com

counseling. *See also* psychotherapists
group, 175
phone, 171–172
couples/partners
massage, 33
worksheets, 22–23
cranial-sacral work, 36, 134, 136, 139, 140, 151
Crary, Elizabeth, 92, 214
cross-reference system, 54
cultural differences and expectations, 126, 128

Dadd, Debra Lynn (*Non-Toxic, Natural and Earthwise*), 110, 153, 154
Defeat Autism Now! (DAN!) doctors, 110, 153, 190, 193
DBT (dialectic behavior therapy), 111
deductive reasoning, definition, ix
depression, 107
causes, 108
in IRI people, 112
medications and nutrition, 109–110, 123
professional help for, 107–108
and sleep patterns, 150
St. John's Wort for, 109
symptoms, 106
in teens, 112, 123
vitamin D for, 109, 153
working with those with IRI
diagnoses, xii
behaviors in medical system, 157
diagnostic manual , 157
differential, 169–170
levels of introverts and extroverts, 13–15
Diagnostic and Statistical Manual of Mental Disorders (DSM-5), 170, 189
dialectical behavior therapy (DBT), 196
divergent thinkers, 61–62
Doidge, Norman (*The Brain That Changes Itself; The Brain's Way of Healing*), 149
down time, 121–122
for parents and partners with IRI, 123–125
for teens, 122–123
for younger/elementary school children, 122
(DSM-5), explaining ADHD, 86
DVDs, 230
anger, 232
sensory issues, 232
social skills, 231
dyspraxia, 142

education. *See also* school staff; teachers
website www.wrightslaw.com
educational kinesiology, 32, 108, 136, 138
electromagnetic frequency (EMF) and radio frequency (RF) exposure, 154–155
EMDR (eye movement desensitization and reprocessing), 108
emotions, identifying in therapy, 172
empathy, and lack of, x, 43–45, 66
ADHD, 86
and confusion, 113
energy medicine, 32, 36, 66, 104, 105, 134, 136, 139, 140, 143, 197
energy psychology, 66, 108, 136, 138, 197
environments. *See* over-stimulating environments
expectations, too high, 91
exposure therapy, 136, 138
extroverts, 9, 11, 13, 16, 26, 185, 241, 245
bipolar, 13
on continuum with introverts, 15
diagnosing, 15
down time needs, 121
eye contact, 26
high, 15–16
low, 15
L3 example, 56
social communication disorder diagnosis, 159
transitioning, 67
eye contact difficulties and tips, 26–29
eye movement desensitization and reprocessing (EMDR), 197

families/family issues. *See also* parents
communication, 125
down time, aiding, 121, 124
and expectations, 128
understanding, and lack, x
working with, 171, 182

fear, 28, 100, 103, 105
    sensory overload, 140
    of talking in front of group, 136
Feelers, 16–19, 20, 27, 38, 242–243
    apologies to Thinkers, 64, 65
    behaviors, 92
    conflict with Thinkers, 64
    examples, 17
    fear response, 100
    Level 3s and 4s, 63
    needs and wants, 18–19
    sadness, dealing with, 94
    teen, 178
    word choice ("I'm sorry"), 64, 65
feelings
    anger, 93
    books about, 97, 105, 227
    defining and identifying, 92, 94, 98, 105
    gladness/glad levels, 94, 97, 98
    mad levels, 5, 98
    overwhelmed, 97
    in relationships, 93
    sadness/sad level, 93–94, 96, 98
    scared feeling and levels, 94, 97, 98
fight-or-flight response, 32, 36, 86, 95, 100, 196
file system, 80–81
filters. *See* sensory issues
504. *See* individual education plan
focus(ing)
    lack, 86–87, 88
    over focus, 84–85
    teen, 118
friends
    books re skills, 228
    making, 9, 10, 13, 56
frustration, 106–107

gaming, 117–119
genetic(s)
    brain wiring, 147–148
    makeup, individual, 25
    vision issues, 151
gifted attributes, 167–169
Gittleman, Ann Louise (*Zapped*), 155
glad levels, 96
grief/grieving, 87, 123, 177, 179, 181, 182, 198–199
    ambivalence stage, 204
    bargaining stage, 203
    crying, anger, guilt, shame, 205–207
    denial, 202–203
    depletion, 211
    depression, 208, 209, 211
    helplessness, 208
    hopelessness, and restoration, 209
    identification, 207
    meaning, relief and restoration, 210
    pain and distress, 203
    phase 1: shock, alarm, denial, and bargaining, 199, 202–203
    phase 2: acute grief 199–200, 202–210
    phase 3: integration of loss and grief, 200–201, 210-212
    regression, 207
    restitution, 210–212
    searching and attempts at retrieval, 204
    unresolved, 212S
grouping similar things, 41–42
guilt and shame, in grieving, 206

health, books, 222–223
help, asking for, 56–57
    from psychotherapist, 60
    steps, 59, 60
highly sensitive people vs. inductive reasoning issues, 143, 144
hormones/hormonal balance and imblance, 109, 110
    addictions, 149
    and brain functioning, 148
    cortisol levels, 110, 150
    gaming affecting, 119
    and sleep imbalances, 150
    teen, 114, 116, 122
hyperactivity, 170

idioms, 128–129, 130, 175, 183, 185
IEP. *See* individual education plan
imagination, often lacking, 69–71
impact on others (of IRI), 47, 51–53
    example, 49–50
    questions, 50–51

impact on others (of IRI) (*continued*)
sentences with blanks, 47–49
social skills, 51–53
individual education plan (IEP), 57–58, 60, 78, 83
time awareness considerations, 84
website wrightslaw.com, 58
inductive reasoning, x, 38
body cues, 4
definitions, ix, 4, 7
and down time, 124
eye contact, 27
lack of, xii, 46, 61
parent lack of, 184
Thinkers, 62
inductive reasoning issues (IRI), x, 4, 46. *See also* body awareness; body language; communication; depression; down time; Levels 1–4; over-stimulating environments; teens
adults/young adults, 79, 86, 88, 117, 178–179
algebra thinking, 163
avoidance of crowds, 26
behaviors, 159–162
books, 213–214
causes, 147
confusion, 113
descriptions/questions by others, 1
details versus larger issues, 4
diagnosing/diagnostic tools, 159, 170
difficulties when out of home, 25
educating them, as important tool, 158
exercise for, 7–8
extroverts vs. introverts, 16
of highly sensitive people, 143, 144
impact on others, 47, 51
information management, difficulty, 26–27
lack of filters, 26
Level 1–Level 4 continuum, 12–13
organizational lack, 5–6
overwhelmed feeling, 6
processing information, 9
severe, 4–5
shutting down, 175
inductive reasoning issues (IRI) (*continued*)
talking loudly/tone of voice, 31–32
thinking predominant over feeling, 19, 20
9thoughts to themselves, 2
understanding, lack, 130
worksheets involving, 20
initiating contact/conversation, 55–56
introverts, 9, 11, 13–14, 16, 26, 185, 241
on continuum with extroverts, 15
down time needs, 121
eye contact, 26
Level 2, 14, 32
Level 3, 14, 32
Level 4, 15
low, 15
parental understanding, 16
taking a role/task, 120
IQ tests, 165–166
IRI. *See* inductive reasoning issues

journaling, 83

Keirsey Bates (*Please Understand Me*), 16, 242
kinesiology, 66, 104 , 151
Kranowitz, Carol (*Out of Sync* and other books), 131 , 134, 141, 214, 215
Kubler-Ross, Elisabeth (grief process), xi, 198

Level 1 IRI (high impact), 9, 12
oversight needs, 9
verbal skills lack, 9
Level 2 IRI (major impact), 9–10, 12, 239–240
brain over focus, 84, 85
extroverts, 14
introverts, 14
jobs for, 10
organization, 81
rules, example, 90
social skills/friends, needs, 9, 12
Level 3 IRI (moderate), 10–11, 13, 240
brain over focus, 84
cross-referencing process, 54, 55
extroverts, 14–15, 56
eye contact lack, 27
feelings, 63
fifth-grade example, 56
initiating conversation, example, 56

Level 3 IRI (moderate) (*continued*)
introverts, 14
logical and/or rigid, 10–11
organization, 81
rules, example, 90
signs of IRI, 159–162
social lacks, 179
sympathy, not empathy, 43
wanting friends, 10
Level 4 IRI, xii, 11–12, 13, 240–241
anxious in social situations, 12
attributes, 167
counseling, 172
cross-referencing process, 54
diagnosing, 159
extroverts, 15
eye contact lack, 27
feelings, 63
goal to blend in, 11
introverts, 15
loneliness, 12
mega-rule, example, 90
organization, 81
perfectionism, 66
social lacks, 179
support needs, 11
sympathy, not empathy, 43
teen difficulty, 11, 59–60, 114
Levine, Mel, parts of attention, 75–76
website www.AllKindsOfMinds.org, 77
licensed marriage and family therapist (LMFT), 171
Linguisystems, 164
literal thinkers, 62–63, 65, 69–70
loss, 199–200. *See also* grief
categories, 201
recovery, 212

mad, levels, 95
massage, 33, 36, 140
McCandless, Jacquelyn (*Children with Starving Brains*), 110, 154
meaning, making and translating, 37, 38, 39–41, 80, 82
"broke the camel's back" example, 37
struggles, 177
Valentine's Day example, 39–40
mega-rules, 68, 70, 79, 80, 81, 82, 88–89, 104
examples, 89, 90
memory, short-term, working, and long-term, 72–73, 74–75
memory-transfer, 73, 78
positives of poor, 74, 75
saving positive pictures, 74
transferring information, 88
visual and auditory, 73
memory transfer issue, 75, 78
movies, 232
Myers-Briggs Type Indicator (for extrovert or introvert determination), 16, 242

nanotechnology, 154
narcissism, x, xii, 158
diagnostic tools, 170
vs. IRI, 169
naturopaths/nutritionists and medications, 32, 74, 87, 109–110, 111, 138, 140, 153, 154
negative thinking, 109, 111, 112
non-verbal learning disorder, 3
notebooks, as helpful, 76
notetaking to aid memory, 72, 76, 80
nutrition
alkaline pH, 151–152
blood type (*Eat Right for Your Type* by Peter J. D'Adamo), 152
gluten and dairy free (GFDF), 153
making your own meals, 153
organic, 152
proper, 109, 131, 138, 141
toxins, 154
vitamin D, 109, 112, 153

obsessive compulsive disorder (OCD), 67–69
demand for routine, 68
diagnosis, 158, 170
example, 68
sensory overload similarity, 140
occupational therapist (OT), 142–143
oppositional defiant disorder, 158
organization, 78, 79, 80–81, 82
of rules, 91

over focus, 84 –85
train example, 85
over-stimulating environments, 135–137, 139
color, 137
sound, 137
taste, 137–138
temperature, 138
texture, 138
overwhelmed feeling, 97

panic/panic attacks, 102–103, 105
parents
behavior expectations for their children, 128
books for, 217
of children with IRI, 87, 179, 183
collaboration with teachers, 58, 83
of depressed children, 112
down time help for their children, 122
extrovert vs. introvert understanding, 16
frustrations with IRI child, 45
gaming supervision, 118–119
grieving over IRI child, 88, 140, 179, 198
groups for, 180–181
with IRI, 123–125, 184
oversight of time habits of young children, 83
support groups, 180
talking/working with children who have IRI, 1–2, 79
teaching specific expectations for their IRI children, 126
of teens, 114–115, 117
working with school staff and psychotherapists, 21
worksheet sharing/involvement, 22, 24
partners of those with IRI, 16, 33, 79, 123–125, 180, 181
past experiences, learning from, 54–55
patience, 8, 41, 46
PDD-NOS diagnosis, 158
perfectionism, 66, 67
David Perlmutter, MD (*Brain Maker*), 109
personality, 55
personality disorder, 157
pillow wrestling, 34, 36
planning and organizing strategies, 76, 83
daily planner, 83
for life after high school, 88
for older children, 87
playing
balancing with work, 84
experienced as controlling, 70
pons tapping or squeezing, 34, 36
pre- and pari-natal shock and trauma, 197–198
priorities, setting, 80
problem solving, 93
psychologist (type of therapist), 190
psychotherapists, 171–173, 187. *See also* coaches; therapists
for adults leaving home and working, 88
crisis management with teens, 178
for depression help, 107–108, 112
diagnosing behaviors and IRI, 157, 158
diagnosing social communication disorder, xii
exploring thinking and feeling, 69
feeling scales, 173
guidelines to follow, 175–176
for negative thinking, 111
perfectionism, help with, 67
scaling in five-point system, 176–177
social skills training, 30
for teens, 59, 60, 115, 116, 123, 178
translating meaning help, 41
for trauma and shock, 109, 188
working with parents and families, 125, 182
worksheets for, 21–22, 23
yes-or-no questions, 172
for young adults, 87
psychotherapy mind and body modalities, 196–197
Brain Gym/educational kinesiology, 197
developmental kinesiology, 197
psychotherapy thinking modalities
cognitive behavioral therapy (CBT), 196
dialectical behavior therapy (DBT), 196
social skills training, 196
puberty. *See also* teens
communication, 114, 116
coping mechanisms, 114
developmental issues, 114

puberty (*continued*)
hormones, 111
parent conflicts, 114–115, 117

questioning
successful, 127, 128, 184–185
"why," 175
quiet time, 104

reactive attachment disorder (RAD), xii, 140, 158, 170
Relaxation and Stress Reduction Workbook, 104, 105
relaxation methods, 33–36, 103–104, 122, 135
breathing, 34–35
calming, 35
gaming, 117, 119
massage, 33
pillow wrestling, 34
pons tapping or squeezing, 34
yoga, 34
remembering, strategies, 80
resistance to change, 67
rewards/praise, 86, 88
Riera, Michael (*Uncommon Sense for Parents with Teenagers*), 92, 115
role taking, 120–121
rules, 68, 70, 77, 79, 80, 81, 82, 86, 88–89, 91, 104

sadness/sad levels, 93–94, 96
safety issues, 144–145
scared/scared levels, 96, 97
school/school staff, 182–183. *See also* teachers
books, 218–219
education about IEPs, 58
parent involvement, 21
speech therapist, 191
worksheets for, 21
searching and attempts at retrieval, in grieving, 204
self-monitoring, 79
sensory integration/ sensory integration therapy, 32, 35, 36, 134, 138, 139, 140
sensory issues/sensory integration disorder (SID), 130
books, 214–215
dyspraxia, 142
postural disorders, 142
sensory discrimination, 142
sensory seeker, 141
under-responsivity, 141
sensory overload/lack of filters, 130–131, 134, 135, 139–140
listening to, 141
smell/taste/texture, 133
sound, 131–132
touch, 132–133
visual/visual overload, 134
sensory processing disorder, diagnostic tests and questionnaires, 166–167
sensory sensitivities/sensory sensitivity issues, 177, 185
sexuality, books, 220
shock, 195–196. *See also* trauma
shyness, 15
siblings and friends, books for, 218
Siegel, Daniel, 92
Simos, Bertha (*A Time to Grieve*), 198
sixth sense and safety, 144–145
sleep issues/sleep apnea, 109, 110, 112, 131, 149–150
CPAP or APAP machines to improve, 151
study, 150-151
supplements (Melatonin, Seraphos, Cortrex, Calms Forte), 150
social anxiety disorder, 15, 26
social communication disorder, x, xii, 3, 158, 159
books, 215
diagnosis, 170
evaluative tools, 163–164
speech therapists, 191
therapists, 180
social interactions/behaviors, 53, 79
cultural differences, 126
literal Thinkers, 62–63
teen, 116, 178
social phobia, x, xii, 15, 26 , 27, 140, 158, 169

social skills/struggles, 15
books, 225–226, 227
communication to improve, 127
and gaming, 119
taking on a role/task, 120
teaching, 126
therapy/books, 70, 111
social skills games, 233
board games, 233–236
online games and resources, 236, 237
social skills training, 196
in groups, 172
social worker (licensed social worker, LSW), 190–191
speech therapists, 30
squeezing, as relaxation technique, 34, 36
strategies, 78
monitoring, 80
note taking, 80
remembering, 80
stress, 105
associated conditions, 98– 99
cortisol effects, 110
down time to relieve, 121
environmental, 119
frustration associated with, 107
gaming to reduce, 119
hormonal imbalance, 109
identifying, 69, 98–99
managing/coping with, 112
in parents with IRI, 123
in social situations, 104
in teens, 114
structural integration, 36, 134, 139, 140-141, 151
students
individual education plan (IEP) or 504, 57–58
in over-stimulating environments, 135
sub-rules, 68, 70, 77, 79, 80, 81, 82, 88–89, 90, 91, 104
support, necessary, xi
sympathy, not empathy, in IRI, 43, 44–45

teachers, 182. *See also* education; school staff
behavior expectations for IRI students, 126
teachers (*continued*)
collaboration/ working with parents, 58, 83
educating about IEPs, 58
expectations and understanding of IRI, xi
extrovert vs. introvert understanding, 16
limited resources, 58
organization help, 81
teaching IEP students how to ask for help, 59, 60
website Counsel-Heal.com, 58
worksheets, sharing, 14
teens (and tweens) with IRI
asking for help, 59–60
body awareness and relaxation suggestions, 33
books, 219–220
chores, 116, 117, 118
colloquialisms, 129
communication, nuanced, 114
depression, 112, 123
developmental issues, 114–116
diagnosing, 15
down time needs, 122–123
focusing, 118
gaming, 71, 117–119
hormones, 114, 116, 122
idioms, 129
inductive reasoning issues, 73, 74, 178
L4s, 59–60, 114
mega-rules, example, 90
memory issues, 73
parent separation, 114–115
psychotherapists working with, 21–22, 115–116, 171
puberty issues, 114
roles/role-taking, 120–121
social cues, difficulty, 114
sub-rules, 91
text language, 129
working with, 178
worksheets for, 22
Temple Grandin Library, 216
tempo control, 78
tension, 36, 99, 107, 111
test-taking, quiet, 86, 88

therapists, types of, 189. *See also* psychotherapists
- chiropractor, 193–194
- Christian, pastoral, or existential therapists, 191
- coach, 191
- DAN! (Defeat Autism Now!) doctor, 193
- licensed marriage and family therapist (LMFT), 189
- licensed mental health counselor (LMHC), 190
- medical doctor (MD), 192–193
- neurologist, 193
- nutritionist, 193
- occupational therapist (OT), 192
- physical therapist (PT), 192
- psychiatrist, 190
- psychologist, 190
- social worker, 190–191
- speech therapist, 191
- vision therapist, 192

therapy, types of
- coping, 194
- emotional, 194
- shock and trauma, understanding, 194–196

Thinkers, 16–19, 20, 242, 243, 245
- conflict with Feelers, 64, 65
- down time need, 122, 125
- emotionally unsupportive, 93
- examples, 17–18
- literal, 62
- needs and wants, 18–19

thinking
- differently, 61–62
- negative, 109, 111, 112

time awareness and management, 82–84
time clock, analog, 83
time constraints, 78–79
Touch for Health, 198
toxins, and clearing, 110, 154
transitions
- as difficult, 35
- preparation for, 67

translating meaning, 39–41
trauma/shock, 109, 148–149, 157–158, 187–188, 194–196
TV suggestions, 233

vaccinations, toxins in, 154
verbal skills, lack, 9, 162–163
video games. *See* gaming
visceral manipulation and structural integration, 36, 134, 139, 140–141, 151
vision issues/therapy, 151, 192
visual information, need to limit, 27, 134
vitamin D, 109, 112, 153

Wi-Fi and cell phone use, 155
Winner, Michelle Garcia (*Social Behavior Mapping; Me Thinking About You Thinking About Me*), 79, 92, 163, 213
word choice (e.g., "I'm sorry), 64, 65
working memory, 72, 73
worksheets, 20–21, 24, 239, 244–249
- couples/partners using/sharing, 22–23
- families/siblings using, 23
- instructions, 239
- levels, 239–241
- psychotherapists using, 21–22
- school staff using, 21
- sharing, 24

worry, and identifying, 69, 99, 100, 103, 105
www.AllKindsOfMinds.org, 77, 80
www.Counsel-Heal.com, xii, 58, 86, 143, 154, 155, 183, 196
www.HomeVisionTherapy, 192
www.InsidetheMind-book.com, 244–249
www.SocialThinking.com
www.wrightslaw.com, 58, 78

yoga, 34, 36
Young, Barbara Arrowsmith, 149
young adults with IRI, 79, 86, 88, 117

Zimmerman, Jack (*Children with Starving Brains*), 110, 154

CPSIA information can be obtained
at www.ICGtesting.com
Printed in the USA
LVHW081328260319
611878LV00031B/677/P

9 781940 598994